CONSERVATIVE HEROES

14 LEADERS WHO SHAPED AMERICA, FROM JEFFERSON TO REAGAN

GARLAND S. TUCKER III

ISI BOOKS

WILMINGTON, DELAWARE

Copyright © 2015 by Garland S. Tucker III
Paperback edition, July 2019

All rights reserved. No part of this publication may be reproduced or transmitted in any form or by any means, electronic or mechanical, including photocopy, or any information storage and retrieval system now known or to be invented, without permission in writing from the publisher, except by a reviewer who wishes to quote brief passages in connection with a review written for inclusion in a magazine, newspaper, or broadcast.

Library of Congress Cataloging-in-Publication Data

Tucker, Garland S.
  Conservative heroes : fourteen leaders who shaped America, from Jefferson to Reagan / Garland S. Tucker ; foreword by Amity Shlaes.
    pages cm
  ISBN 978-1-61017-157-1 (paper)
  1. Conservatives—United States—Biography. 2. Conservatism—United States—History. 3. Right and left (Political science)—United States—History. 4. United States—Politics and government. I. Title.
  JC573.2.U6T84 2015
  320.52092'273—dc23
                                            2015007845

Published in the United States by

ISI Books
Intercollegiate Studies Institute
3901 Centerville Road
Wilmington, Delaware 19807-1938
www.isibooks.org

Manufactured in the United States of America

CONSERVATIVE HEROES

For
Grey and Liza
and the next generation

Contents

FOREWORD
    Tucker's Gift
    by Amity Shlaes   9

INTRODUCTION
    "A Faithful Band"   17

1   Thomas Jefferson and James Madison
    Founding Collaborators   27

2   Nathaniel Macon and John Randolph
    The "Tertium Quids"   45

3   John C. Calhoun
    "The Cast-Iron Man"   61

4   Grover Cleveland
    Character and Courage   77

5   Calvin Coolidge and Andrew Mellon
    Commonsense Government   97

6   Josiah W. Bailey
    The Conservative Manifesto of 1937   119

7   John W. Davis
    "Public Enemy Number One"   137

8   Robert A. Taft
    "Mr. Republican"   157

9   William F. Buckley Jr., Barry Goldwater,
    and Ronald Reagan
    The Conservative Triptych   173

EPILOGUE
    "As Old as the Republic Itself" 201

Notes 203

Acknowledgments 219

Index 221

Foreword

TUCKER'S GIFT

BY AMITY SHLAES

Years ago a junior senator decided to write a book about his predecessors. The senator belonged to the Democratic Party, as his father, also a name in politics, had done before him. Yet the senator determined that he would not produce a party tract or a partial history. He would make a study of all kinds of senators, however controversial. He would describe both Democrats and Republicans, and he would bust stereotypes. The theme the author chose was political integrity—the integrity of breaking with the pack when one's conscience demanded it, and the more subtle integrity of personal sacrifice for the group.

The senator-author was John Fitzgerald Kennedy. The book was *Profiles in Courage*. One disputed chapter in the book covered Robert Taft of Ohio. Taft, who had recently died, was not just any Republican. Taft was Senate majority leader, and was so associated with the GOP that he was nicknamed "Mr. Republican." After World War II Taft had taken the deeply unpopular step of opposing the Nuremberg Trials. Taft's critics went after him relentlessly: "his heart bled anguishedly for the criminals at Nuremberg," a colleague commented. Yet, as Kennedy noted with admiration, Taft had stuck to his position, for the Ohio senator could not see how retroactive justice could be justice at all.

Precisely because it was so fair, *Profiles in Courage* won a Pulitzer Prize and became a bestseller whose relevance abides today. Taft's challenge to retroactive justice comes up in considerations of jurisprudence regarding both suspected al-Qaeda terrorists and Saddam Hussein. Even those who cannot sanction Taft's position can find utility in Kennedy's book.

So will it be with *Conservative Heroes*, Garland Tucker's own volume of profiles in courage. As Kennedy did, Tucker dares to choose hot topics and to depict his heroes unconventionally. Tucker, for example, reclaims Thomas Jefferson as a conservative, not a move of which today's Jefferson-shy Grand Old Party is likely to approve. And as Kennedy did, Tucker illuminates not only his subjects' integrity but also their flaws, even when fatal.

Another hero is John W. Davis, a figure obscured by modern history books because he argued on the side of states' rights, and therefore against desegregation, in a companion case to 1954's *Brown v. Board of Education*. Yet as Tucker shows, Davis accomplished too much to dismiss him simply as a bigot. The West Virginian determined early on to make a difference through the law: while still a student he told his peers that an attorney could be "the sentinel on the watchtower of liberty." Over his career Davis proved not merely a jurist, but a great one: *Brown* was not the first but the 140th case that Davis argued before the Supreme Court. In a 1952 case, *Youngstown Sheet and Tube Co. v. Sawyer*, Davis convinced even some of the progressives on the bench that the federal government's seizure of steel-production facilities was unconstitutional.

Some readers will be surprised to find that Davis also took the initiative at many times to help blacks—and paid for that help dearly. While Davis was solicitor general in Woodrow Wilson's administration, he defended black voting rights before the Supreme Court—and won. The Democratic Party that nominated Davis for president in 1924 was the party of the Ku Klux Klan. Yet Davis denounced the Klan explicitly over the course of the campaign, saying that the Klan "must be condemned by all those who believe, as I do, in American ideals." In such a declaration Davis outclassed his Republican opponent, Calvin Coolidge, who remained silent on the Klan. This bold stance cost Davis support and even, some wager, the election. But Davis's move set a new standard for decency on race in our political process.

Similar bravery was, however, demonstrated by Coolidge on a different field: fiscal policy. Today our conception of a hero president is that of an active executive, changing the country from Washington. Coolidge demonstrated a rarer kind of heroism: that of restraint, whether restraint of himself or of Congress. While in office, Coolidge vetoed the entitlements of his day, farm support and support for veterans. He allowed bills to die in recess, a move known as the pocket veto. Often he did not even comment on his own inaction.

Such behavior has often been depicted as laziness, or cruelty, or both. When Coolidge died, the commentator Dorothy Parker asked, "How can they tell?" Yet Coolidge's refusal to grant entitlements to various groups came out of strength and a confidence that all citizens would benefit if only the government did not favor one faction.

Tucker adds value by sketching out Coolidge's greatest campaign, a campaign to cut taxes. Together with Treasury Secretary Andrew Mellon, Coolidge fought to restore tax rates to pre–World War I levels. This endeavor was not easy, especially because Mellon and Coolidge found an opponent in an increasingly progressive Congress. To get lawmakers to agree to lower rates even modestly, Mellon and Coolidge initially had to concede a condition they regarded as deeply offensive to American freedom: the tax authorities could publicly release the returns of top taxpayers. Yet Coolidge and Mellon persevered, managing, within a couple of years, to reverse the heinous "public returns" rule. They also successfully pressured Congress to reduce top tax rates to levels below not only those of Woodrow Wilson and Franklin Roosevelt but also those of Dwight Eisenhower and Ronald Reagan. Today the Coolidge top tax rate of 25 percent sets the bar for Republican presidential candidates.

Marvelously, Tucker carries the tax story forward, showing how Josiah Bailey of North Carolina and other little-known skeptics, many Democrats, pressed back when the New Deal threatened to engulf the private sector. The "Conservative Manifesto" that Bailey led the group in publishing inspired small-government fans and provided the template for the Republicans' 1994 Contract with America.

Most debated in Tucker's roster will be John C. Calhoun, born in 1782. Like nearly all of his southern peers, Senator Calhoun supported slavery, and explicitly so. This has been enough to see him wiped out from children's texts. Yet the omission leaves younger citizens in the dark about some valuable history. For example, Calhoun became the leading opponent of the tariff, a protectionist measure that benefited some parts of the country at the expense of others. He maintained his opposition even when it threatened his own political ambitions. In 1832 Calhoun resigned the vice presidency rather than continue to serve under President Andrew Jackson, who refused to reduce the so-called Tariff of Abominations. Calhoun's opposition led to compromise that reduced tariff rates, benefiting all consumers and establishing the virtuous Democratic Party tradition of lower tariffs. In *Profiles in Courage*, and later on the presidential campaign trail in 1960, Kennedy expressed his "admiration for this great South Carolinian" and praised the "courage of Calhoun in refusing to repudiate" positions that were unpopular, or even tragically wrong. "I never know what South Carolina thinks of a measure," Calhoun once said. "I act to the best of my judgment and according to my conscience." Of South Carolina, Calhoun added: "If she approves, well and good. If she does not, and wishes anyone to take my place, I am ready to vacate. We are even."

Taken together, Tucker's profiles remind us that America is broader than we think, and that the country's history is too subtle to force into the framework of modern progressivism. These accounts underscore two other points often skipped over. The first is that supporting states' rights is not equivalent to supporting racism. The second is that American conservatism was not born with Fox News, as much as Tea Party opponents pretend. Our traditional respect for states' rights and restrained government run back to the American Revolution. After all, many of our revolutionaries considered themselves the conservatives, defenders of rights once honored in England but now abused by the arbitrary George III.

Many readers resent the narrowness standard histories offer. They will welcome *Conservative Heroes*, which so thoughtfully draws out the full picture. This book will also broaden both college and high school syllabi.

Not all will select the same heroes Tucker does. No matter. History is "an argument without end," wrote the historian

Pieter Geyl. Tucker's gift is to supply Americans with facts and stories that enable us to participate better in the great argument.

Amity Shlaes *is the author of four* New York Times *bestsellers,* Coolidge, The Forgotten Man: A New History of the Great Depression, The Forgotten Man (Graphic Edition), *and* The Greedy Hand: Why Taxes Drive Americans Crazy.

CONSERVATIVE
HEROES

Introduction

"A FAITHFUL BAND"

Looking back on his early years in politics as a conservative, former secretary of war Newton D. Baker recalled, "I was one of a faithful band fighting a hopeless battle for a philosophy as old as the Republic itself."[1] That political philosophy was originally called "classical liberalism" but now more often is termed "conservatism." For much of this country's history, "liberalism" connoted a belief in the maximum personal freedom consistent with the maintenance of order. But twentieth-century progressives "changed the English language," as author Amity Shlaes points out.[2] With the rise of the New Deal, liberalism became synonymous with increased centralization of power in government—always justified in the name of greater equality and justice. By the second half of the twentieth century, that "faithful band" resisting the growth of government commonly went by the name "conservative," particularly after the publication of Russell Kirk's *The Conservative Mind* (1953) and Senator Barry Goldwater's bestseller *The Conscience of a Conservative* (1960).[3]

This book endeavors to identify and trace the development of American conservatism from the founding of the Republic into the modern era by examining the lives and writings of fourteen important figures—some lesser known than others, but all of real significance. It in no way purports to be a comprehensive survey of American history or a definitive study of the individuals included. But examining these leaders allows us to bring the foundational principles of conservatism into sharper relief and see how those principles have been put into action over time.

Conservatism's Foundational Principles

Over the past century, most historians have viewed American history through the philosophical lens of modern progressivism. These historians have lionized leaders who expanded the role of government and sought to implement programs designed to redistribute private property, control markets, and otherwise put Washington in charge.

Consider Arthur Schlesinger Jr., one of the most prominent historians of the twentieth century. Schlesinger's sons have written of their father, "He was always in some way promoting and advancing the liberal agenda; it was his mission, purpose, and justification."[4] Schlesinger himself wrote that a liberal is one who "believes that the mitigation of economic problems will require a renewal of affirmative government to redress the market's distortion and compensate for its failures."[5] Historian Thomas Silver, in *Coolidge and the*

Historians, wrote: "In the hands of a historian like Arthur Schlesinger Jr., history becomes a weapon. It is wielded in the fight to advance a political cause."[6] And Schlesinger was hardly alone. Henry Steele Commager, Allan Nevins, Doris Kearns Goodwin, and many other liberal historians have shaped much of the perspective on American history.

Take, for example, the mainstream interpretation of the politics and economics surrounding the Great Depression. Nevins and Commager dismissed the Republican-dominated 1920s as "dull, bourgeois, and ruthless," portrayed Calvin Coolidge as a do-nothing president who was subservient to business interests, declared that the "New Deal was long overdue," and praised Franklin Roosevelt for meeting the crisis "with boldness and vigor."[7] For his part, Schlesinger hailed Roosevelt as the nation's "savior"—a president who was always "for action, for forward motion, for the future."[8]

There has, however, been a resolute minority of historians who have upheld a conservative view. This group includes writers like Paul Johnson, Clinton Rossiter, Niall Ferguson, Russell Kirk, and Amity Shlaes. In stark contrast to Nevins and Commager, Johnson hailed Coolidge as "the most internally consistent and single-minded of American presidents" and concluded that "Coolidge prosperity was huge, real, and widespread."[9] Shlaes and others have documented how the New Deal didn't end the Great Depression but in fact prolonged and exacerbated it—how, as Shlaes put it, "government intervention helped to make the Depression Great."[10]

This book is situated unabashedly in the conservative camp. It treats conservatism seriously as a political philosophy and shows how its foundational principles have remained consistent throughout American history. I believe the following five concepts have proved to be of fundamental importance:

First, conservatism is grounded in a realistic view of human nature. Conservatives believe there is nothing in human history to suggest the perfectibility of man. Though created by God in the divine image, man is a fallen creature in need of redemption. Left to his own devices, he reverts to violence, dissolution, and aggression. Patrick Henry and other Founders spoke often of "the depravity of human nature."[11] In *Federalist* No. 6 Alexander Hamilton warned, "Men are ambitious, vindictive, and rapacious."[12] This view of human nature keeps conservatives from accepting the progressive notion that mankind inevitably advances and improves. The divide between conservative and progressive worldviews was evident as early as the Founding. The American Revolution was, in fact, "a revolution not made but prevented," as Russell Kirk put it—the American Founders saw themselves as *restoring* the traditional rights of Englishmen. The French Revolution, by contrast, "utterly overturned the old political and social order."[13] Kirk explained the "principal difference" between these two so-called revolutions: "The American revolutionaries in general held a biblical view of man and his bent toward sin, while the French revolutionaries in general attempted to substitute for the biblical understanding an optimistic doctrine of human goodness advanced by the philosophes of the rationalistic Enlightenment. The American view led to the Constitution of 1787; the French view, to the Terror and to a new autocracy."[14] Conservatives thus believe that the American Republic was founded not to reform human nature but rather to establish the boundaries within which human nature might flourish.

Second, because of man's fallen nature, the primary roles of government are to establish order and preserve liberty. There is a definite tension between these roles, and the conservative would generally advocate the *maximum* degree of personal liberty while maintaining the most *basic* level of order. As we shall see, this debate began early in American history, as Thomas Jefferson, James Madison, and other Founders argued over various elements of the Constitution. The threat of anarchy was real in the early days of the Republic, but there also loomed the fear of a repressive, centralized government. The same tension was at the heart of the dissolution of the Union during the Civil War. In the mid-twentieth century Senator Robert A. Taft practiced "the 'Great Tradition' of politics: maintaining justice through a healthy tension of order and freedom."[15] Conservatives have recognized the need for order but have been wary of government encroachment on personal liberty. They have refused to equate any and all changes with desirable reform. Hasty innovation and disregard for precedent are not the path to real progress.

The third canon is closely linked to the second. The conservative stops abruptly at those two primary roles of government. There is no important third role, for the scope of government is to be limited. Jefferson spoke for most of the Founders when, in his first inaugural address, he said: "A wise and frugal Government, which shall restrain men from injuring one another, shall leave them otherwise free to regulate their own pursuits of industry and improvement, and shall not take from the mouth of labor the bread it has earned. This is the sum of good government."[16] The Founders feared that any governmental power that extended beyond the barest protection of liberty could itself become a threat to liberty. Jeffersonians saw local institutions as the common man's best protection against the threat of a strong central government.

Fourth is a conviction that property rights and human rights are inseparably bound together. The Founders were well grounded in John Locke's views on the rights of property.

As Paul Johnson has written, all the Founders "derived from John Locke the notion that security of one's property was intimately linked to one's freedom."[17] John Adams wrote, "Property must be secured, or liberty cannot exist." Hamilton concurred: "Adieu to the security of property, adieu to the security of liberty."[18] In the twentieth century John W. Davis affirmed this same truth: "The chief aim of all government is to preserve the freedom of the citizen. His control over his person, his property, his movements, his business, his desires should be restrained only so far as the public welfare imperatively demands. The world is in more danger of being governed too much than too little."[19]

In a new nation forged out of the wilderness by the initiative of pioneers, there was no concept of economic equality—neither as a reality nor as a goal. Madison denounced any "equal division of property" as "improper" and "wicked."[20] In observing American democracy in the 1830s, Alexis de Tocqueville cautioned that "democratic institutions strongly tend to promote the feeling of envy" and "awaken and foster a passion for equality which they can never entirely satisfy." Tocqueville also warned that there exists "in the human heart a depraved taste for equality, which impels the weak to attempt to lower the powerful to their own level, and reduces men to prefer equality in slavery to inequality with freedom."[21] That is why securing property rights is so important: doing so, wrote the political scientist James Q. Wilson in the twentieth century, provides "perhaps the most powerful antidote to unfettered selfishness."[22] For the conservative, an individual should be free to strive, invest, and achieve without fear that his rewards will be seized and without envy of his neighbor's success. As we shall see, the link between property and liberty has remained a cornerstone of conservative thought throughout American history.

Fifth, the social and political life of a community and a country depends on private virtues. The Marxist critic Granville Hicks once wrote contemptuously, "The Tory has always insisted that, if men would cultivate the individual virtues, social problems would take care of themselves."[23] There is more than a grain of truth in that. The great eighteenth-century British statesman Edmund Burke, often called the father of modern conservatism, wrote: "But what is liberty without wisdom, and without virtue? It is the greatest of all possible evils."[24] Conservatives throughout history have believed that virtues flow from a particular culture—a culture based on Judeo-Christian virtues. As Russell Kirk wrote: "Burke does not approve of religion because it is a bulwark of order; instead, he says that mundane order is derived from, and remains a part of, divine order. Religion is not merely a convenient myth to keep popular appetites within bounds."[25] The men profiled in this book all valued this culture and its traditions. And they lived political and personal lives of civility and integrity, as even their political opponents attested.

Fourteen Leaders

In the following chapters, we turn to the lives of fourteen leaders who defended and advanced the tenets of American conservatism. The story begins with the friendship and collaboration of Jefferson and Madison during the formation of the Republic and in their opposition to the Federalist program. Both men ascended to the presidency—and once in office, both partially abandoned their strict interpretations of the Constitution. Their "Old Republican" principles were carried forward in Congress by Nathaniel Macon, John Randolph, and the "Tertium Quids." In the next generation, the torch was passed to John C. Calhoun, one of the greatest political thinkers in American history. Although basic Jeffersonian principles became hopelessly entangled in the sectional battle over slavery during this period, Calhoun's writings and speeches on federalism versus government centralization contributed greatly to the foundation of conservatism.

With the Civil War came unparalleled centralization of power in Washington and a long period during which Jeffersonian thought was little heeded. In a backlash against big government and corruption, Grover Cleveland was elected president in 1884, returning Jeffersonian principles to power. With a combination of courage, character, and common sense, Cleveland effected conservative reforms and stood for sound money and a free market. He served two terms but ultimately lost control of his party to William Jennings Bryan and the progressives, as the country began a twenty-five-year, bipartisan love affair with progressivism.

After the exhilaration of Teddy Roosevelt's and Woodrow Wilson's progressive administrations, and the exhaustion of the Great War, the country returned to "normalcy" under President Warren Harding. The restoration of Jeffersonian principles began with Harding, but it accelerated when his sudden death in 1923 brought to power his vice president, Calvin Coolidge. Over the next five years, President Coolidge and his treasury secretary, Andrew Mellon, reduced the size and scope of the national government, reduced the tax burden, and thus fostered the free-market conditions that produced an economic boom. Theirs was a record of principled conservative governance.

When the stock market crashed in 1929 and the Great Depression began, Coolidge's Republican successor, Herbert Hoover, ignored conservative principles and instead turned toward government intervention. Then Franklin Roosevelt entered office and took this interventionism to unprecedented levels. The embrace of federal government power to solve all problems came to define modern liberalism. And American conservatism began to redefine itself as the alternative to modern liberalism. Defenders of limited government, federalism, free markets, and individual liberty—concepts that the New Deal had seemingly written off—resisted the extraordinary centralization of power. The conservative challenge emerged in Congress, first under Democratic leaders such as Josiah W. Bailey and then under a revival of the GOP as the conservative party led by Robert A. Taft, and before the courts with the brilliant advocacy of John W. Davis.

World War II postponed the political reckoning for the failed liberal policies of the 1930s, but the postwar period witnessed the ascendance of conservatism. First, William F. Buckley Jr. and his *National Review* brought vigorous conservative thought to the mainstream. Buckley influenced politicians like Barry Goldwater and Ronald Reagan, and he inspired countless young people to rally around the conservative banner. By 1964, Goldwater and the conservatives had seized control of the GOP from liberal Republicans. Goldwater's crushing loss to President Lyndon Johnson that fall led most pundits to proclaim that conservatism could never be a serious political force. But Reagan brought conservatism to commanding heights with his sweeping victory in 1980. His historic presidency "changed the trajectory of America," as even President Barack Obama has acknowledged.

This "faithful band" has provided a rich and honorable history for twenty-first-century conservatives. In examining the lives and careers of these leaders, we honor the wisdom of Winston Churchill, who reminded us, "We cannot say 'the past is the past' without surrendering the future."[26]

1

THOMAS JEFFERSON AND JAMES MADISON

Founding Collaborators

The fifty-year friendship of Thomas Jefferson and James Madison provided the basis for a political collaboration that profoundly affected the burgeoning American republic. Through the struggle for American independence, the formulation and adoption of the Constitution, the Federalist years, and the Virginia ascendancy, these two friends conferred, debated, and defined the basic tenets of constitutional conservatism; they also plotted the practical, political implementation of these principles. Their surviving correspondence numbers some 1,250 letters and provides a remarkable window into the early years of the nation. Both were products of the Virginia aristocracy—well born, well educated, and well versed in the principles of John Locke, Edmund Burke, and the English Whigs. They were in basic agreement that the two primary purposes of government were to ensure order and to preserve liberty. But they often differed on how best to achieve the necessary balance between these two often conflicting objectives.

Jefferson expressed far more confidence in democracy, local (and state) government, and the rationality of the people, while Madison tended to support the federal government's protection against undisciplined local majorities, the inviolability of private property rights, and the restraining hand of government on the excesses of the people. They both advocated limited government, but each drew the line at a different point. Jefferson was ever the philosopher, whereas Madison more often served as the voice of practical politics. In studying their correspondence over the constitutional debate and during the Federalist period—especially over the Kentucky and Virginia Resolutions—one can see two distinct political minds struggling to find common ground. Theirs proved to be not only an amiable friendship but also an extremely fruitful philosophical and political partnership. This chapter focuses on only one short period of their long collaboration (1787–1798), but it was a period that greatly affected American conservatism.

"I Am Not a Friend to a Very Energetic Government"

Jefferson and Madison met in 1776, when both were elected to serve in the Virginia House of Delegates. Madison, just twenty-five, was a newcomer to politics, whereas Jefferson, the elder by eight years, had spent several years in the predecessor body, the House of Burgesses, and would soon be elected governor of Virginia. There was no question initially as to who was the senior partner, but Madison's serious, scholarly nature soon established him as coequal. By the end of Jefferson's controversial term as governor in 1781, Madison had emerged as a leading defender of the beleaguered Jefferson. His spirited defense cemented their friendship before Jefferson's departure in 1784 as U.S. minister to France. Both men had labored under the hopelessly ineffective Articles of Confederation and had become convinced of the need for thorough constitutional reform. Wartime improvisations were no foundation upon which to build a nation.

From Europe, Jefferson provided Madison with a steady stream of letters covering everything from the Greco-Roman theory of republican government to practical advice concerning the various thirteen American states. Meanwhile, Madison was engaged in the daily give-and-take of practical politics as a member of the Confederation Congress. He had been reelected in 1786 despite term limits that prohibited congressmen from serving more than three out of every six years. It was in the fall of 1786 that a potentially dangerous uprising of debt-ridden farmers in western Massachusetts erupted under the leadership of one Daniel Shays. After forcing the state supreme court to flee Springfield in terror, the ruffians seized control of the state arsenal. Cowering before this ragtag mob, the legislature rescinded direct taxation. The powerlessness of the Confederation was clearly exposed, and the public cry for constitutional change began to rise.

Madison wrote urgently to Jefferson seeking his assessment of Shays's Rebellion. Jefferson responded nonchalantly that it did "not appear to threaten serious consequences," but Madison labeled the rebellion treason and called for "vigorous actions" to put it down.[1] On March 18, Madison wrote to George Washington, "It would seem that a calm has been restored [in Massachusetts].... The precautions taking by the

State, however, betray a great distrust of its continuance."[2] Madison clearly viewed Shays's Rebellion not only as an ominous sign but also as an effective argument in urging constitutional reform. Decades later he would recall that "a crisis had arrived which was to decide whether the [American] Experiment was to be a blessing to the world, or to blast forever the hopes which the republican cause had inspired."[3]

In fact, Madison had already been convinced of the need for reform. Shays's Rebellion represented only the most "recent and alarming" example of the shortcomings of the Articles of Confederation. Madison had conceived the Annapolis Convention, which convened in September 1786, less than two weeks after the rebellion broke out in Massachusetts. Ostensibly called to discuss interstate trade, the Annapolis meeting quickly moved to the topic of amending the Articles of Confederation.

It was at Annapolis that Madison first began to strategize with Alexander Hamilton. Hamilton was the leader of an emerging group of "federalists," most of whom were prominent New York and Philadelphia businessmen. They had repeatedly attempted—with no success—to amend the Articles of Confederation to establish a sound, national financial structure. Although their philosophical underpinnings were different from Jefferson's and Madison's, the federalists became natural allies in the development and ratification of the Constitution. In February Madison wrote to Washington, "I am inclined to hope that they will gradually be concentered in the plan of a thorough reform of the existing system."[4]

The Annapolis Convention produced a resolution, drafted by Madison and Hamilton, making a perspicaciously broad appeal to have delegates from all the states reconvene in Philadelphia in May "to devise such further provisions as shall appear to them necessary to render the constitution of the Federal Government adequate to the exigencies of the Union."[5] With this sweeping, self-proclaimed authorization, the delegations convened in Philadelphia.

After attending to several housekeeping rules, including the election of Washington as presiding officer, the delegates began serious debate on what came to be known as Madison's "Virginia Plan." Because Madison was a decidedly uninspiring speaker, he had asked fellow Virginian Edmund Randolph to introduce the plan.

On May 29, Randolph offered the fifteen resolutions that comprised Madison's plan for a national government of three branches—an executive, a judiciary, and a two-house legislature. It was clear from the outset that the Virginia Plan was not a narrow revision of the old Articles but rather the creation of a significantly more robust national government. The legitimacy for this government was derived directly from the people rather than from the states—hence the carefully selected phrase "We the people."

Once Randolph had presented the plan, Madison set to work as the recognized author and floor leader, participating extensively in the ensuing six-week debate. Madison here exhibited his penchant for thorough preparation and meticulous groundwork. In a letter to Washington some weeks before the convention, he outlined the major provisions of the plan with this introduction: "Conceiving that an individual independence of the States is utterly irreconcilable with their aggregate sovereignty; and that a consolidation of the whole into one simple republic would be as inexpedient as it is unattainable, I have sought for some middle ground, which may at once support a due supremacy of the national authority, and not exclude the local authorities wherever they can be subordinately useful." After describing the various checks and balances in his proposed national government, Madison concluded with this critical element: "To give a new System its proper validity and energy, a ratification must be obtained from the people, and not merely from the ordinary authority of the Legislatures."[6] Washington's crucial support was forthcoming, although it was subtly delivered throughout the convention with his habitual, Olympian reticence and seeming impartiality.

As the Philadelphia convention began its serious work, Madison wrote apologetically to Jefferson that a code of silence had been adopted. Jefferson objected vigorously: "I am sorry they began their deliberations by so abominable a precedent as that of tying up the tongues of their members."[7] From the outset, Madison's Virginia Plan set the agenda for the secret debates. William Pierce, delegate from Georgia, wrote, "What is very remarkable about him is that every person seems to acknowledge his greatness. He blends together the profound politician with the Scholar."[8] Madison has thus become known to us as the "Father of the Constitution."

In October, after adjournment of the convention, Madison penned a momentous seventeen-page letter to Jefferson with which he enclosed a copy of the Constitution. Here he provided a history of the convention, his own analysis of the Constitution, and his vision of future political life in the new republic. He reported on four central goals of the convention's deliberations:

> 1. To unite a proper energy in the Executive, and a proper stability in the Legislative departments, with the essential character of Republican Government. 2. To draw a line of demarcation, which would give to the General Government every power requisite for general purposes, and leave to the States every other power. 3. To provide for the different interests of different parts of the Union.

4. To adjust the clashing pretensions of the large and small States.[9]

Madison then tackled the central question of limiting the role of the national government. He emphasized to Jefferson that the new federal government rested squarely "on the people"—not on the state legislatures. He also underscored the narrow limits placed on national authority. Madison's attention to these points almost certainly indicated his suspicion that Jefferson would be concerned by the scope of the "new system."

Jefferson was indeed concerned on that score. Writing to John Adams about his misgivings, Jefferson confessed to have found "things in it which stagger all my dispositions."[10] He clearly believed the convention had overreacted to the fear of anarchy and rebellion, and he feared the heavy hand of an overly powerful central government.

In a letter of December 20, 1787, Jefferson offered Madison his thorough analysis of the approved Constitution—its shortcomings but also its merits. In signaling his reservations, Jefferson was among the first to advocate a bill of rights "providing clearly and without the aid of sophisms for freedom of religion, freedom of the press, protection against standing armies, restriction against monopolies, the eternal and unremitting force of the habeas corpus laws, and trials by jury in all matters of fact triable by the laws of the land and not by the law of nations." Jefferson saw this bill of rights as "what the people are entitled to against every government on earth." Also, he expressed concern over the failure to limit expressly the tenure of the president. Some of the federalists were advocating lifetime tenure, but Jefferson recognized potential danger and requested clarity. In addition to these two specific concerns, Jefferson underscored to Madison his underlying general suspicion of government. In classic Jeffersonian language, he prophetically warned, "*I own I am not a friend to a very energetic government. It is always oppressive.*" Here Jefferson sought to separate Madison from his federalist allies and, in so doing, laid one of the cornerstones of American conservatism.[11]

Despite his concerns, however, Jefferson expressed support for many aspects of the constitutional plan. He began his analysis by telling Madison, "I like much the general idea of framing a government which should go on of itself peaceably, without needing continual recurrence to the state legislatures." He was quick to single out as "inviolate the fundamental principle that the people are not to be taxed but by representatives chosen immediately by themselves." Predictably, Jefferson offered hearty approbation of the democratic aspects of the plan. He was "captivated by the compromise of the opposite claims of the great and little states" in the bicameral legislature. Also, he voiced support for the dispersion of power into the three branches.[12]

Jefferson retained some doubts about the new Constitution. The correspondence between Jefferson and Madison from this time highlights their shared principles but also where the two friends departed. For example, the two friends held opposing views about the role of the states. Madison thought the states were excessively—even dangerously—democratic, whereas Jefferson took comfort in democratic majority rule in the states. They also differed on the question of political stability. Jefferson wrote to Abigail Adams, "I like a little rebellion now and then."[13] Such cavalier comments made Madison wince. In the end, though, they came to agreement on the Constitution. Madison secured Jefferson's support for it, in particular by assuring his friend of the appropriateness of a bill of rights.

Securing the approval of the necessary states was now the immediate challenge. On October 27, 1787, an essay advocating adoption of the new Constitution appeared under the pseudonym Publius in three New York newspapers. Over the next ten months, another eighty-four Publius essays were published. They sought unflinchingly to address the antifederalist concerns and advance the federalist points of persuasion. This body of writing, now known as *The Federalist Papers*, has been accorded historical constitutional significance second only to the Constitution itself. Many years later it was revealed that the three authors of this series were James Madison, Alexander Hamilton, and John Jay.

In *Federalist* No. 10, Madison addressed the threat of partisan faction and insurrection—the need for government to provide order. He wrote, "The latent causes of faction are thus sown in the nature of man." The purpose of government, he concluded, is to control *the effects* of human nature—not to eliminate liberty or to change human nature. In *Federalist* No. 14, Madison made the case for a limited national government: "The general government is not to be charged with the whole power of making and administering laws. Its jurisdiction is limited to certain enumerated objects." He amplified this point in No. 45:

> The powers delegated by the proposed Constitution to the federal government are few and defined. Those which are to remain in the State governments are numerous and indefinite. The former will be exercised principally on external objects, as war, peace, negotiation, and foreign commerce; with which last the power of taxation will, for the most part, be connected. The powers reserved to the several States will extend to all the objects which, in the ordinary course of affairs,

concern the lives, liberties, and properties of the people, and the internal order, improvement, and prosperity of the State.

Anything not specifically enumerated was reserved for state and local government. In *Federalist* No. 39, Madison identified the source of authority for formation of the federal government and simultaneously defined its limits: "Each State, in ratifying the Constitution, is considered as a sovereign body, independent of all others, and only to be bound by its own voluntary act. In this relation, then, the new Constitution will, if established, be a FEDERAL, and not a NATIONAL constitution."[14]

The authors of *The Federalist Papers* were hardly omniscient. In No. 45, Madison predicted, "The number of individuals employed under the Constitution of the United States will be much smaller than the number employed under the particular States"—a prediction sadly rendered inaccurate in the subsequent decades. Similarly, in No. 46, Madison stated: "The members of the federal will be more dependent on the members of the State governments, than the latter will be on the former."[15] Few twenty-first-century state governors would concur. Underlying these inaccurate predictions, however, was the Founders' assumption of limited powers for the federal government.

After being published in New York, the *Federalist* essays were rapidly disseminated into other states. The impact of the *Federalist* on the ratification debate in New York was decisive, but the wider impact was more difficult to determine. The essays certainly framed the debate, which the federalists ultimately won: the necessary nine states had ratified the Constitution by June 1788, and the other states would eventually follow suit. Even more important, the *Federalist* essays have served as an invaluable aid to legal scholars and judges in discerning the original intent of the Founders.

The Birth of Strict Constructionism

With the Constitution ratified, Madison and Jefferson turned to the task of breathing life into the newly created structure. Madison was elected to serve in the First Congress (he barely defeated another future president, James Monroe). He urged the new president, George Washington, to choose Jefferson—who returned from France in the fall of 1789—as the first secretary of state, and then he cajoled his friend into accepting the post. Madison wrote to Jefferson "that further light must be added to the Councils of our Country" before their republican philosophy would be broadly adopted.[16]

It was not long before the philosophical battle lines began to form within the new government. Treasury Secretary Alexander Hamilton and Vice President John Adams sought a general strengthening of the national government, while Jefferson and Madison resisted concentration at every turn. Hamilton's fiscal schemes culminated in his formal recommendation of a national bank in late 1790. Hamilton defended his proposal under a broad interpretation of "implied powers" in the Constitution. Madison and Jefferson roundly rejected that interpretation. It was clear to them that nothing in the Constitution granted to the federal government the power to form a national bank and that, therefore, the power to incorporate banks was reserved to the states.

In early 1791 the Virginia compatriots took the lead in denouncing the bank measure. On February 2, Madison gave a speech on the floor of Congress in which he declared that the bill was "condemned by the silence of the Constitution."

The Constitution gave the federal government the authority to make laws "necessary and proper" to carry out the powers expressly granted to it. "The proposed bank," Madison said, "could not even be called necessary to the government; at most it could be but convenient." If the bank plan was approved, he said, "the essential characteristic of the government, as composed of limited and enumerated powers, would be destroyed."[17] Only two years into Washington's first term, Madison, the "Father of the Constitution," was now convinced that the great democratic victory might be lost.

Less than two weeks later, on February 15, Jefferson declared his opposition to Hamilton's bank bill directly to President Washington. In a letter to the president, he wrote, "The incorporation of a bank, and the powers assumed in this bill, have not, in my opinion, been delegated to the United States by the Constitution." Noting that proponents of the bank claimed authority in the Constitution's "general welfare" clause, Jefferson pointed out that according to that clause, "they [Congress] are not *to do anything they please* to provide for the general welfare, but only to *lay taxes* for that purpose." To interpret that clause as broadly as Hamilton wanted would, Jefferson concluded, render Congress the "sole judges of the good or evil" and thus provide "a power to do whatever evil they please."[18] He foresaw a powerful national government that would provide political and economic protection to speculators, manufacturers, developers, and businessmen, while trammeling on the precious liberty of the majority of Americans.

Here was born a struggle between strict and broad interpretations of the Constitution—a struggle that has continued unabated for more than two centuries. Madison and Jefferson laid the philosophical bedrock of American conservatism in their opposition to the Federalist policies.

They could not defeat Hamilton's bank plan, however. President Washington, after considering his cabinet's advice on the constitutionality of the bank measure, signed the bill into law. The law granted the Bank of the United States a twenty-year charter that would require congressional approval for renewal.

Losing that battle—and thus seeing a loose construction of the Constitution prevail—only intensified Madison's opposition to Hamilton, the Federalists, and any efforts to increase the power of the federal government at the expense of the people and the states. He wrote a series of fiery newspaper articles to arouse "the public mind." Only vigilant local government manned by an educated, engaged electorate could counter the trend toward overweening national government, he said. In January 1792 he challenged "every citizen" to be "an Argus to espy, and an Aegeon to avenge," assaults on America's freedom.[19] He took his argument to the floor of Congress on February 6:

> If Congress can apply money indefinitely to the general welfare, and are the sole and supreme judges of the general welfare, they may take the care of religion into their own hands; they may establish teachers in every State, county, and parish, and pay them out of the public Treasury; they may take into their own hands the education of children, establishing in like manner schools throughout the Union; they may undertake the regulations of all roads. In short, everything from the highest object of State legislation, down to the most minute object of police, would be thrown under the power of Congress.[20]

These were prophetic words that would become the warning of successive generations of conservatives.

"The Chains of the Constitution"

With Washington's decision to return to Mount Vernon at the end of his second term, the young nation faced its first contested presidential election. Jefferson and his Republicans were arrayed against John Adams and the Federalists. Under the early constitutional provisions, the leading candidate in the Electoral College, Adams, was elected president, while the runner-up, Thomas Jefferson, was elected vice president, thus ensuring a heated continuation of the Washington-era battles.

The partisan conflict intensified as Adams's administration faced a crisis in foreign policy. Despite efforts to maintain independence, America was continually drawn into the conflict between Britain and France. In general, Adams's Federalist administration sought to distance itself from the French Revolution and sympathized more with Great Britain, whereas Jefferson's Republicans were pro-French. The European powers were eager to force the Americans to take sides. Foreign policy thus became a defining issue for the two parties. President Adams and his Federalists launched an unofficial war with France over France's efforts to meddle in internal U.S. politics. The so-called Quasi-War saw naval clashes in the Caribbean between American commercial ships and French naval vessels. To protect against French meddling on the American frontier, the Federalists authorized a standing army, which infuriated the Jeffersonians.

The divide separating the parties grew even wider in 1798, when the Federalist-controlled Congress passed and President Adams signed four bills that became known as the Alien and Sedition Acts. These acts extended the national government's power to imprison and to deport aliens, whom the president deemed "dangerous to the peace and safety" of the country, and also to restrict speech that was "false, slanderous, and malicious" and that brought "contempt" upon the government.[21] Federalists supported these laws under the banner of national security, but the Republicans saw the acts as an unconstitutional extension of federal power. There ensued a massive public outcry, which Jefferson and Madison assiduously nurtured over the next two years.

The strident partisan warfare over the Alien and Sedition Acts produced a defining chapter in American conservatism. The central issue was: what is the proper role of the federal government versus that of the states? The principle of judicial review by the Supreme Court had not yet been established; that would come in 1803, with the landmark decision in the case of *Marbury v. Madison*. Therefore, Madison and Jefferson turned to the states to challenge the federal government's usurpation of power. Their efforts culminated in the passage of the Kentucky and Virginia Resolutions.

In 1798 Jefferson secretly drafted a set of resolutions about the Alien and Sedition Acts that the Kentucky legislature passed. His Kentucky Resolutions declared that "unless arrested at the threshold," the Alien and Sedition Acts would "necessarily drive the states into revolution and blood." In these resolutions, Jefferson blasted the federal government as a tyranny that desired to govern with "a rod of iron." He predicted that failure to stop the national government would result in the "annihilation of the state governments." Free government, he argued, "is founded in jealousy, and not in confidence." The people must jealously guard their rights against any unauthorized usurpation by the government. Jefferson called on the states, as representatives of the people, to demand a halt to these dangerous federal acts. He famously added, "In questions of power, then, let no more be heard of confidence in man, but bind him down from mischief by the chains of the Constitution."[22]

Perhaps most important, Jefferson's Kentucky Resolutions declared the Alien and Sedition Acts "void and of no force." It was here that the term *nullification* entered the American political lexicon, suggesting a most extreme doctrine of states' rights. It was not entirely clear whether Kentucky alone was nullifying the acts or rather calling upon its fellow states to rise up with Kentucky to nullify them. In any event, the term stuck and would be the seed of great controversy in the next generation.[23]

Keep in mind that Jefferson was the sitting vice president in the very government he was condemning. Had his role in drafting the Kentucky Resolutions been known, he might have been charged with treason.

Madison, meanwhile, wrote the resolutions that the Virginia legislature passed. Like the Kentucky Resolutions, the Virginia Resolutions forcefully condemned the Alien and Sedition Acts, although Madison's language was somewhat more temperate than Jefferson's. He labeled the acts "unconstitutional" rather than "void," and he introduced the theory of "constitutional modes of interposition by the States against abuses of powers." Historians, politicians, and legal experts have parsed these words carefully ever since, seeking to discern the intent of Madison's *interposition* and Jefferson's *nullification*.[24] Certainly, interposition was less radical than nullification. It is generally held to mean that the interposer—in this case the states—acts as an instrument of the people to bring pressure on the government to pull back within the bounds of the Constitution. In later years, as the sectional debate over slavery threatened to rend the Union, Madison was quick to distance his earlier call for interposition from any form of nullification.

In any event, the purpose of these resolutions was to rally state governments into protest against federal laws that exceeded a strict reading of the Constitution and to move the balance of power away from the national government. In the immediate term, Jefferson and Madison failed in their efforts: the other states did not follow Kentucky and Virginia in challenging the federal government on the Alien and Sedition Acts.

But the public outcry they generated proved sufficient to oust the Federalists from power. In the "Revolution of 1800," as Jefferson delighted in terming it, the Republicans swept into power in the nation's capital, with Jefferson winning the presidency and his party taking control of nearly three-quarters of the seats in the House of Representatives. Jefferson's Republicans soon repealed one of the intolerable acts and let the others expire. But the great debate over the role of the federal government would continue—not just through Jefferson's presidency but for centuries to come.

"The Sum of Good Government"

The great friendship and collaboration between Thomas Jefferson and James Madison continued well into the nineteenth century. Madison served as President Jefferson's secretary of state throughout Jefferson's two terms. He then succeeded his friend as president, with the retired Jefferson providing a steady stream of advice from Monticello. When Madison retired as president in 1817, the two Founders continued their collaboration until Jefferson's death in 1826. The proximity of their Virginia homes afforded frequent personal visits, and their written correspondence continued as before.

Over the years, the responsibilities of governing wrought changes in both men's views on the role of government. Jefferson famously abandoned his strict constructionist philosophy in securing the Louisiana Purchase. As we shall see in the next chapter, members of Jefferson's own party charged the president with abandoning the "Republican principles of 1800." As president, Madison endured similar attacks from "Old Republicans" when he seemed to back away from his earlier pronouncements on strict constructionism—when, for example, he supported rechartering the Bank of the United States and expanded federal responsibilities for building roads and canals. But Jefferson and Madison would not be the last leaders to face such concerns. Indeed, conservatives have often been more principled in opposition than in governing.

Despite the challenges associated with putting principle into action, the contributions of Jefferson and Madison have proved fundamental to American conservative thought. Their writings in the earliest years of the republic serve as foundations for the conservative view that the Constitution carefully restricts the federal government's powers—that, as Madison put it, it is the "essential characteristic" of the federal government to be "composed of limited and enumerated powers." Later defenders of Jeffersonian principles would develop a maxim often (but probably mistakenly) attributed to Jefferson: "That government is best which governs least."[25] Even if Jefferson never uttered those words, his belief in limited government was unmistakable. Recall his first inaugural address, which clearly articulates his vision of the role of government. Jefferson said: "Still one thing more, fellow citizens—a wise and frugal government, which shall restrain men from injuring one another, shall leave them otherwise free to regulate their own pursuits of industry and improvement, and shall not take from the mouth of labor the bread it has earned. This is the sum of good government, and this is necessary to close the circle of our felicities."[26]

2

NATHANIEL MACON AND JOHN RANDOLPH

The "Tertium Quids"

When Jefferson's and Madison's Republicans swept into power in the election of 1800, the party faced a new challenge: governing. The Federalist Party had previously held a majority in the House of Representatives, but after the "Revolution of 1800," Republicans held 103 of 142 seats. Reorganizing the leadership of the House became an immediate priority.

In 1801 the House elected Nathaniel Macon of North Carolina as Speaker. In organizing the House leadership, Macon turned to his close friend and political ally John Randolph of Virginia (a cousin of Thomas Jefferson) to chair the critically important Ways and Means Committee and serve as the Republicans' floor leader in the House. These two statesmen have fallen into relative obscurity, but together they wrote an all-important chapter in the history of American conservatism.

An Unlikely Friendship

Nathaniel Macon was born into a prominent Huguenot family whose forebears came to America from France after the Catholic king revoked the Edict of Nantes in 1685. The family first settled in Williamsburg, Virginia, and later migrated to northeastern North Carolina, along the Roanoke River in what became Warren County. Nathaniel was born in 1757 near Warrenton, North Carolina, and attended the College of New Jersey (later Princeton University). He served in the American Revolutionary army as a private, twice refusing election as an officer. After serving in the North Carolina House, where he opposed ratification of the Constitution as an undue impingement on sovereignty of the states, Macon was elected to the U.S. House of Representatives in 1791. He quickly gained recognition as a competent and reliable member of the anti-Federalist party. In 1794–95 Macon joined with James Madison in strongly opposing the Jay Treaty, a treaty of "amity, commerce, and navigation" with Great Britain that the pro-French Jeffersonians saw as too favorable to the British.

Likewise, in 1798 Macon took a forceful stand in the heated debates over the Alien and Sedition Acts. He took to the floor of the House to denounce the measures, warning that if Congress could suppress the liberty of the press, it might well pass a law establishing a state religion. He added: "Laws of restraint, like this, always operate in a contrary direction from that which they are intended to take. The people suspect something is not right when free discussion is feared by the government."[1] Macon went on to support the Kentucky and Virginia Resolutions and to urge North Carolina's adoption of a similar resolution. It was in this debate that Macon voiced his view that the federal government existed by virtue of the limited powers granted by the states, saying: "This [federal] government depends upon the State Legislatures for existence. They have only to refuse to elect Senators to Congress and all is gone." He ended the speech by expressing his hope that the Supreme Court would ultimately declare the act unconstitutional.[2] The principle of judicial review by the Supreme Court was not established until 1803.

By 1800, Macon's vision of a limited national government was well established and well articulated. Therefore, it was natural that Jefferson and Madison should have supported his election as Speaker with enthusiasm. Macon had gained the support and respect of many others as well. He was plain-spoken, honest, and straightforward: that rare politician without guile. Historian John Wheeler wrote in 1851: "Macon was emphatically and radically a democrat. He was willing to trust the people further than Jefferson would have ventured, far beyond Washington, and to an extent that Hamilton would have pronounced anarchical."[3] Biographer William E. Dodd said, "He was, by sheer force of character and by ten years of unflinching consistency, the leader of the House."[4]

In 1799 Macon met John Randolph, a first-term congressman from Virginia, who resided farther up the Roanoke River from Macon's North Carolina home. Randolph was in personality and temperament Macon's absolute opposite, yet politically they were in close alignment. They became the closest of friends and remained so throughout their careers. Sixteen years younger than Macon, the twenty-six-year-old Randolph cut quite a figure in Washington. As Dodd wrote, "John Randolph was a man who could not pass through a street without attracting all eyes to himself."[5] A contemporary gave this description: "His long thin legs, about as thick as a stout walking cane, were encased in a pair of tight, small clothes, so tight they seemed part and parcel of the limbs. Handsome white stockings were fastened at the knees by a small gold buckle." Instead of the traditional fan-tailed coat, Randolph wore a more dramatic swallow-tail coat. He wrapped a large white silk cravat around his neck. His complexion "was precisely that of a mummy; withered, saffron, dry, and bloodless." His eyes were "impulsive and passionate, with an expression at times such as physicians describe as that of insanity. I never beheld an eye that struck me more."[6] An avid fox hunter, Randolph often strode onto the floor of the house in riding attire followed closely by his hounds.

Randolph and Macon struck up a friendship when Macon rose to offer a resolution to reduce funding for the army. Defenders of a larger appropriation, he said, "think borrowing five or six millions a trifling thing." But such borrowing was "unjust," he declared, in an admonition that conservatives have echoed down through the decades: "If we contract a debt we ought to pay it, and not leave it to your children. To be sure it is much easier to vote money than to lay taxes, because people do not directly feel the vote, but if taxed they must instantly know it."[7] After Macon spoke these words in his usual straightforward manner, the young John Randolph rose to offer his support. In what was to become a familiar congressional spectacle, Randolph captivated the House with his wit, sarcasm, and inimitable manner. A spectator observed that the Federalists winced as Randolph ridiculed "the loungers, who live upon the public, who consume the fruits of their honest industry under the pretext of protecting them from a foreign yoke. They [the people] put no confidence, sir, in the protection of a handful of ragamuffins."[8]

Here was Congress's first glimpse of what this unlikely

friendship would produce over the next twenty-five years: Macon, the steady, experienced, thoughtful, well-liked, and well-respected leader of the House complemented by his mercurial, caustic, brilliant, and flamboyant friend. Two more different personalities it would be impossible to imagine, yet they were united on principle. They believed in economy in government, strict constructionism, state sovereignty, and individual liberty.

Although Randolph had served only one term in Congress before Macon's election as Speaker of the House in 1801, Macon, with Jefferson's assent, appointed the talented young Virginian to chair the House Ways and Means Committee and be the Republican floor leader in Congress.

Rolling Back Government

With Jefferson as president, Madison as secretary of state (functioning virtually as copresident), Macon as Speaker, and Randolph as House floor leader, the Republicans were determined (in Dodd's words) "to give this country such a government as had never been seen any where, a government as simply conducted as a country debating society."[9]

Indeed, Republican simplicity was the order of the day. All Federalist affectations of grandeur were banished: no levees, no carriages, no grand state dinners, no liveried servants. Jefferson set the tone by riding solemnly on horseback to the Capitol for his inaugural. The president immediately proposed reducing annual government expenses from $7.5 million to $3.5 million, and the Republican Congress duly passed the legislation over the outraged cries of the Federalists. Expenditures were slashed, and the retirement of the national debt became a priority.

Congress quickly turned to repealing the Judiciary Act of 1801 and John Adams's "midnight appointments." In early 1801 the lame-duck Federalist Congress had passed the act to increase the number of federal courts, and President Adams appointed Federalist judges to fill the new positions right up to the eve of Jefferson's inauguration. The Federalists forecast dire consequences if these new courts were abolished, but Randolph countered that doing so would not only save money but also "give the death blow to the pretension of rendering the judiciary a hospital for decayed politicians."[10] Within a year, the Republican-controlled Congress had repealed the 1801 act and passed a new law organizing the federal judiciary.

In the early days of Jefferson's first term, Congress briefly debated how to reapportion representation in the House based on the recently completed national census. This debate explored the very meaning of representation. Randolph advanced a position that he and Macon would champion until their retirement. He declared that members of the House were representatives not of the people but of the *states*. A New England Federalist countered that he was as much a representative of Virginia as Randolph, since the House formed "a great national body, designed for national purposes." Randolph scoffed at this suggestion. He and Macon saw themselves as citizens of their respective sovereign states, serving as representatives to a national government that was strictly limited by the Constitution.

Later in Jefferson's first term, Macon and Randolph confronted an issue that would become a more obvious cause of the Civil War: slavery. After some years of quiet neglect, the question of slavery reached the House floor in 1804 when a bill proposed to levy a tax on the importation of slaves, which South Carolina had reinstituted. Macon opposed any reopening of the slave trade, but he was more alarmed by what appeared "to be an attempt in the General Government to correct a State for the undisputed exercise of its constitutional powers."[11] When the resolution was introduced on the floor of the House, Macon referred it to the Ways and Means Committee, where Randolph ensured that it was postponed indefinitely.

This incident appears to mark the first stand Macon or Randolph took on the question of slavery versus the rights of the states. It is important to trace the development of Macon's and Randolph's views on this, the most divisive issue in American history. In 1797 Macon called slavery a "curse" but said he saw "no means of getting rid of it." A slaveholder himself, he believed that abolishing slavery would create chaos. In short, his views on slavery were of his time and place.

Randolph, by contrast, opposed slavery on principle. His stepfather, St. George Tucker, wrote *A Dissertation on Slavery* (1796), which began with an epigraph from Montesquieu: "Slavery not only violates the Laws of Nature, and of civil Society, it also wounds the best Forms of Government; in a Democracy, where all Men are equal, Slavery is contrary to the Spirit of the Constitution."[12] Randolph owned slaves, but in 1826 he wrote, "From my early childhood, all my feelings and instincts have been in opposition to slavery in every shape."[13] Unlike Jefferson, Randolph was ultimately true to his instincts. In his will he freed his slaves and provided land for them in the free state of Ohio. Sadly, Ohioans greeted the former slaves with violence and drove them from the land Randolph had purchased for them.

In his biography of Randolph, Russell Kirk wrote, "To slavery he was opposed on principle all his life; but he saw it as a problem almost insoluble in the South, and he prepared, with increasing sternness, to wall it away from external interference."[14] Macon, while holding more standard proslavery views, adopted a similar position when it came to federal attempts to interfere with slavery. When the question of the tax on the importation of slaves came up in 1804, Macon began his response by saying that "the morality or the immorality of the slave trade had nothing to do with the question before the House." He continued: "Gentlemen think that South Carolina has done wrong in permitting the importation of slaves. That may be, and still this measure [the tax] may also be wrong."

Thus we see, as early as 1804, the Jeffersonian principles of a limited national government and the sovereignty of state and local governments applied in defense of noninterference with slavery. In the coming decades, and especially by John C. Calhoun's time, this position would become the keystone in the South's defense of slavery.

Rift

Macon and Randolph heartily approved of Jefferson's radical reversion to limited government. Early in Jefferson's presidency they advanced the administration's program through Congress, their contrasting styles evident throughout. Presiding over the House as Speaker, Macon employed evenhanded leadership, for which he retained bipartisan respect. Meanwhile, as Russell Kirk wrote, "Randolph ruled the House literally booted and spurred, the master of the new Republican Congress as much from terror as from love, and congressmen hastened to obey his edict."[15] They embraced the principles of 1800, which they understood to be simplicity and economy in government, individual freedom from economic and political oppression, and forbearance and peace in foreign affairs.

But Macon and Randolph became increasingly uneasy as

Jefferson and Madison moved toward a more expansive view of government. The first indication of Macon's dissatisfaction appeared in 1803 in a letter to James Monroe in which he criticized the administration's "purchasing" policy—that is, the Louisiana Purchase, which aroused serious concerns about its constitutionality. But Macon's language was guarded, and his criticism was aimed at Madison rather than Jefferson.[16] He would not long remain so cautious in his criticisms of the administration.

Randolph, characteristically, was far less guarded. He vociferously opposed the Louisiana Purchase as unauthorized by the Constitution. As early as 1805, in a typical outburst of hyperbole, Randolph declared, "The Louisiana Purchase was the greatest curse that ever befell us."[17] He foresaw the coming clash for territory between the agrarian, slaveholding South and the commercial North.

Neither Randolph nor Macon would abide a politician who strayed from the strict constructionist principles that had brought him to power. As the historian Henry Adams noted, "These old republicans of the South . . . always asserted their right to judge party measures by their private standard, and to vote as they pleased."[18]

In 1804, as floor leader of the Republicans in the House, Randolph led the impeachment of Supreme Court justice Samuel Chase, a staunch Federalist who was charged with allowing his political partisanship to influence his rulings. The House voted to impeach Justice Chase, and Randolph then led the prosecution in the Senate, which the Republicans controlled, and over which the Republican vice president, Aaron Burr, presided. To Randolph's dismay, some Republican senators joined Federalists in voting to acquit Chase. Randolph became so outspoken in his opposition to the president that it rendered him ineffective as chairman of the Ways and

Means Committee, and in 1805 Macon—who was reelected Speaker with a bare majority—did not reappoint him.

No longer chairman of Ways and Means, Randolph appeared now as leader of a small band of "Old Republicans" who became known as *Tertium Quids*—the third things. "He never tired of using his brilliant oratory to nettle the Administration," as one historian put it. "Randolph was indeed a voice crying in the wilderness, but with all his eccentricity he did represent the emergence of a desire on the part of some elements in the South to return to the strict-constructionist principles of 1798."[19] The rift in the Republican Party widened in 1807, when Macon failed to be reelected Speaker and joined the Quids in open opposition to the Jefferson administration.

The Tertium Quids fought consistently for "purity and economy in government, peace and prudence in foreign relations, and freedom from economic oppression by special interests," in the words of Russell Kirk.[20] They stood with Macon in his passion for economy in government—he called it "commonsense" government—which ensured that every substantial appropriations bill was met by "the severest, sharpest, most stringent and constant refusal," as a biographer remarked. With Macon, "not only was parsimony the best subsidy, but the only one."[21] The Quids also stood with Randolph when he declared that "change is not reform" and when he laid out the following as "a cardinal principle" for all statesmen: "never, without the strongest necessity, to disturb that which is at rest."[22] They equally stood with the Virginian in his belief that, as Kirk phrased it, "a democratic passion for legislating is a menace to liberty." Kirk offered a succinct summary of Randolph's view on the subject: "When a people begin to think that they can improve society infinitely by incessant alteration of positive law, nothing remains settled: every right, every bit of property, every one of those dear attachments to the permanence of family, home and, countryside is endangered."[23]

"This Government Was Intended to Be a Limited One"

For Macon, Randolph, and the Republicans, one of the festering controversies involved the very issue that had so exercised Jefferson and Madison in the earliest days of the Washington administration: the federally chartered Bank of the United States. By Jefferson's second term, the bank was well into its congressionally authorized twenty-year charter, and the Republicans eagerly awaited their chance to kill it in 1811. Randolph on more than one occasion likened the Bank of the United States to a house of ill repute. He considered the bank unconstitutionally chartered and established for the benefit and protection of a minority at the expense of the majority. Years later Macon expressed the dominant Old Republican view: "Banks are the nobility of the country, they have exclusive privileges; and like all nobility, must be supported by the people and they are the worst kind, because they oppress secretly."[24] The campaign against the Bank of the United States succeeded: in 1811 the Republicans narrowly defeated the rechartering of the bank. But the victory would prove short-lived.

An equally defining issue was the tariff, another measure Hamilton introduced early in Washington's administration. As they did with the Bank of the United States, the Quids argued that the Constitution did not permit the federal government to impose a tariff, which protected one group of citizens at the expense of another group. Macon and Randolph fought—and lost—numerous tariff battles over their long congressional tenure, but their concept of free trade became a great conservative principle and would ultimately achieve wide acceptance more than a century later. Late in his career, during one of the last tariff battles he would fight, Macon wrote to his son-in-law, Weldon Edwards: "I have heard that the tariff would be taken up today or tomorrow in the House. We must wear old clothes, and put patch on patch, and not be ashamed, provided we owe nothing, though we may not be dressed in the fashion, there is no better fashion, than to be out of debt."[25]

Macon and Randolph viewed the expanding scope of the national government and the seductive lure of federal deficits as dangerous threats to liberty. Randolph warned: "If ever the people of this country lose their liberties, it will be by sacrificing some great principle of government to temporary passion. There are certain great principles, which if not held inviolate, at all seasons, our liberty is gone."[26] To Macon and Randolph, the appropriations schemes appeared endless, and the American propensity to legislate change seemed constant.

At every turn the Quids were opposing some new extension of federal power—with less and less success each time. In 1816 Congress chartered the second Bank of the United States over strident objections from the Quids. Macon, Randolph, and the Quids had been reduced to a tiny faction; the Republican Party had come to embrace the Bank of the United States and other extensions of federal power that were anathema to the principles of 1800. As early as 1811, Randolph had lamented the abandonment of true Republican principles. Old Republicans could no longer be found, he said: "Death, resignation, and desertion had thinned their ranks. They had disappeared. New men and new doctrines had succeeded."[27] In an 1828 letter, Macon wrote: "Almost every bill reported is to take money out of the Treasury. It must be thought by some that a public debt is a public blessing and all who live on the public, no doubt think, the more taxes the better, and that every tax adds to industry; from such I wish to be delivered."[28]

Macon and Randolph fought a rearguard action through the Jefferson and Madison years and beyond, displaying a consistency rarely seen in American political life. In 1815 Macon was elected to the Senate from North Carolina, and Randolph joined him there in 1825. Late in his career, Macon took to the Senate floor to oppose a canal project with these words: "I rise with a heavy heart to take this last farewell of an old friend—the Constitution of the United States. My heart is full when I think of all this; and what is to become of us I cannot say. This government was intended to be a limited one; its great objects were war and peace and now we are endeavoring to prove that other objects are necessary."[29]

"These Doctrines Did Not Perish"

The lives and careers of Nathaniel Macon and John Randolph hold one of the most important chapters in the history of American conservatism. Though opposites in style and temperament, they remained dedicated to the same fundamental principles throughout their more than three decades in Congress. Together they defined and articulated the most basic tenets of conservatism, which they called the "Republican principles of 1800," and together they ensured that these principles survived. As Russell Kirk wrote, "These doctrines did not perish; they were guarded, battered but obdurate, and were passed on to later generations who gave them a more hearty welcome than they had long experienced."[30]

Despite his long career in Congress, the caustic, erratic Randolph did not always enjoy political success: he never regained the leadership position in the House he enjoyed early in his career, and he even lost a bid for reelection in 1812 (he was elected again in 1814). But, as Henry Adams wrote, "it would be folly to question the abilities of a man who, at twenty-six," could so captivate the House. "The proof of his genius lies in his audacity, in the boldness with which he commanded success and controlled it."[31] In defending and advancing conservative principles, Randolph laid a philosophical foundation upon which later generations of conservatives built. Indeed, twentieth-century American conservatives came to recognize his views on limited government, the rights of states, individual liberty, and human nature as fundamental. Russell Kirk wrote, "Perhaps nothing else in American political philosophy is more brilliant than are Randolph's greatest speeches."[32] Understanding Randolph's view of human nature helps us understand conservatism's moral underpinning. He viewed man as corrupt, and therefore he believed an individual's best hope lay in a government severely limited in power to prevent exploitation by evil men. Randolph, whom Kirk called an "aristocratic libertarian," rejected Jeffersonian notions of equality, defiantly exclaiming: "I am an aristocrat. I hate equality. I love liberty."[33]

Upon his retirement in 1828, it was said of Macon that "in his nearly forty years in Congress, no ten members gave as many negative votes." A close friend of Macon once said, "If Mr. Macon should happen to be drowned, I should not look down the current for his body, *but up the stream!*" The historian John Wheeler marveled that "no plan, however specious, no device however artfully contrived, no scheme however plausible, swerved his steady mind from his firm purpose." Yet, unlike Randolph, Macon compiled this uninterrupted history of opposition without expressing or eliciting any rancor. "His opposition was open, his reasons plain, and his intercourse frank and pleasant," Wheeler wrote. "He often spoke in Congress, always agreeable and amiable, but firm and always opinionated."[34] Randolph declared in his will that "Mr. Macon was the wisest and best man" he had ever known, and Jefferson said that with Macon's death the republic would mark the passing of *Ultimus Romanorum*—the "last of the Romans."[35]

Unlike Randolph, Macon was reelected without interruption and was revered by the voters of his state for his character, temperament, and principles. Over his career, he could claim never to have campaigned for office, never to have attended a party caucus, and never to have offered patronage to any man. Consistent to the end, Macon requested that his grave be marked simply—and inexpensively—with a pile of stones, gathered by family and friends from his fields. His wish was granted, and a massive mound of stones, which admirers have augmented over the years, still marks the grave. In 1919, however, the state of North Carolina erected a handsome stone marker detailing Macon's long years of service to his state—yet another small confirmation of the expanding role of government. *Mr. Macon would not have approved!*

3

JOHN C. CALHOUN

"The Cast-Iron Man"

On February 28, 1827, John C. Calhoun confronted an agonizing choice. As the sitting vice president, Calhoun had strategically maneuvered before the Senate a tariff bill designed simultaneously to forestall substantial tariff increases and to advance his party's political designs at the expense of the opposition Whigs. But the Senate vote did not split along the lines anticipated; instead it had resulted in a deadlock. As president of the Senate, Calhoun would cast the tie-breaking vote.

Calhoun was widely seen as a serious contender for the presidency. After entering Congress in 1811, he had made a name for himself as the most brilliant debater in the House. Under President James Monroe he had served ably as secretary of war. As vice president under John Quincy Adams, the

South Carolina native was popular and well respected not just in the South but throughout the country. But now this tie-breaking vote threatened his national ambitions and even his reputation at home. A vote against the tariff bill would seriously damage Calhoun's standing with the pro-tariff northerners whose support he would need for a presidential run. Meanwhile, a vote for the measure would economically cripple the South and his native South Carolina.

Calhoun, despite entering Congress as a Jeffersonian Republican, was on record as pro-tariff. He was a fervent nationalist who early in his congressional career had supported Henry Clay's "American System" of internal improvements and tariffs, including the Tariff of 1816. That tariff, which many southerners had supported, was not radically protective, but the rates had increased in subsequent years, contributing to widespread economic suffering in the South. In 1816 southerners sold their cotton for twenty-seven cents per pound; by 1827 the price had fallen to only nine cents per pound. The proposed tariff increases would only add to the South's economic hardship.

For years, the brilliant, flamboyant, and largely ineffective John Randolph had railed against the tariff as one of many unhealthy signs of federal consolidation. As early as 1816, Randolph had attacked the "tariff humbug" as a serious threat to his state and region. He said that the North, which by then wielded a majority in Congress when coupled with the West, "preferred industry to agriculture as 'progressive.'"[1] He saw the tariff issue as but one of those constituting a surrender of sovereignty by the states. Any such surrender was dangerous to Randolph: "To ask a State to surrender part of her sovereignty is like asking a lady to surrender part of her chastity."[2] Few in the South joined Randolph in sounding the alarm—certainly not Calhoun.

But as presiding officer of the Senate, Calhoun had witnessed many of Randolph's denunciations of the tariff. Randolph's brilliance and eloquence appealed to Calhoun's intellectual nature. Gradually, the certitude and optimism of Calhoun's early political convictions eroded, and he began to brood on the dangers to his state and region—and to his beloved Union. The voluble, erratic, emotional, and romantic Randolph had found in the stately, self-controlled, disciplined, and consistent Calhoun a grudging convert and worthy heir.

And so on February 28, 1827, Calhoun made his first public move against the tariff—and his first step down the path of Randolph's strict constructionism. He cast the dramatic tie-breaking vote to defeat the tariff.

Instantly Calhoun was thrust to the forefront of the tariff debate. He began to speak out publicly on the issue. Although there was already heated talk of disunion, Calhoun had no sympathy for such emotional excess. He believed the tariff laid a heavy economic burden on the South while transferring wealth to the North and West, but his objective was constitutional reform, not secession. In writing to Postmaster General John McLean, Calhoun warned: "One section will be bribed by means flushed from another. The industry of a favorite section will be promoted by the sacrifice of another."[3] Some weeks after the vote, he rose in South Carolina to make this toast: "The Constitution of the United States—intended for the protection and happiness of the whole, may it never be perverted into an instrument of monopoly and oppression."[4]

"THE ESSENCE OF LIBERTY"

Events of the following year thrust Calhoun further into the fray with the introduction of the Tariff of 1828, infamously known in the South as the "Tariff of Abominations." The Republicans—by now known as Democratic-Republicans, and soon to be simply Democrats—again sought to finesse the issue. Party leaders hoped to splinter support for the bill, which would result in sustaining the existing tariff levels while leaving their presidential candidate, Andrew Jackson, with support from both sides. (Jackson had already proved a master at working both sides of this divisive issue.) The plan appeared to be working as the tariff bill narrowly passed the House and was sent to the Senate. Here they expected New England senators to kill the bill, which included amendments that raised duties on raw materials vital to New England industry. That would allow southerners to avoid any increase in taxes but also to blame northerners for defeating the bill. As it happened, New England senators supported the tariff, which raised most duties from 30 percent to 50 percent. The bill passed, and President John Quincy Adams, despite his deep misgivings, signed it.

South Carolina exploded in protest against the tariff. The state's political leaders and planters besought Calhoun to find a constitutional solution. Senator Robert Y. Hayne was prepared to take the fight to the floor of Congress, and much of the congressional delegation fell in behind him. Many South Carolinians were openly talking of disunion.

Passage of the Tariff of Abominations truly shocked Calhoun. His biographer Margaret Coit wrote: "His first horrified look into the abyss had been too clear; in a glance he had seen impending civil war or the dissolution of the Union, and to a man of his patriotism, these alternatives were equally horrible."[5] As would slavery in the near future, the tariff divided the country into sections, and this sectionalism posed a dire threat to the Union. Randolph's warnings now haunted Calhoun. He wrote to a friend of the tariff, "It was worse than folly; it was madness."[6]

But Calhoun's first priority was to elect Jackson president in 1828 with the hope that he would be receptive to tariff reduction. Consequently, Calhoun's writings and speeches during the campaign months were muted on the tariff question. He was not ignoring the issue, however. In fact, he spent the next six months ruminating over it. As he did so, he became convinced that the problem was broader than just the tariff; there was, he concluded, "a fatal disease lurking in the system."[7]

In November, Andrew Jackson won a decisive electoral victory, 178–83, and Calhoun was easily reelected vice president, with support from Pennsylvania, New Jersey, Ohio, and Kentucky in addition to his southern base.

In December, Calhoun anonymously sent a ninety-page essay on the tariff question to the special committee of the South Carolina House of Representatives. The essay, which has come to be known as the "South Carolina Exposition and Protest," argued for limiting government in order to preserve liberty and to protect a minority of the country from the arbitrary, capricious will of the majority. Calhoun wrote: "Stripped of all its covering, the naked question is whether ours is a federal or a consolidated government; a constitutional or absolute one; a government resting ultimately on the solid basis of the sovereignty of the States or on the unrestrained will of a majority; a form of government, as in all other unlimited ones, in which injustice, and violence, and force must finally prevail."[8] He pointed out that this was a matter not for South Carolina alone but for every state, region, and class. If the absolute power of the majority were established, then the security of all was endangered.

Calhoun harked back to the Founders' insistence on limited government. He quoted Madison's arguments in the *Federalist* and embraced the logic of the Kentucky and Virginia Resolutions. He wrote:

We have acted, with some exceptions, as if the General Government had the right to interpret its own powers, without limitation or check; and though many circumstances have favored us, and greatly impeded the natural progress of events, under such an operation of the system, yet we already see, in whatever direction we turn our eyes, the growing symptoms of disorder and decay—the growth of faction, cupidity, and corruption; and the decay of patriotism, integrity, and disinterestedness. In the midst of youth, we see the flushed cheek, and the short and feverish breath, that mark the approach of the fatal hour; and come it will, unless there be a speedy and radical change—a return to the great conservative principles which brought the Republican party into authority, but which, with the possession of power and prosperity, it has long ceased to remember.[9]

Much of the South Carolina Exposition was devoted to analyzing the economic and political effects of the tariff. Calhoun believed the tariff heavily benefited the northern manufacturing states to the detriment of the agricultural South:

> The duty on imports, which is mainly paid out of our labor, gives them the means of selling to us at a higher price; while we cannot, to compensate the loss, dispose of our products at the least advance. It is then, indeed, not a subject of wonder, when understood, that our section, though helped by a kind Providence with a genial sun and prolific soil should languish in poverty and sink into decay, while the rest of the Union, though less fortunate in natural advantages, are flourishing in an exampled prosperity.[10]

Calhoun clearly discerned the resulting crisis: "The interest of the two great sections is opposed. We want free trade—they restrictions; we want moderate taxes, frugality in Government, economy, accountability, and a rigid application of the public money to the payment of debt, and to the objects authorized by the Constitution. In all these particulars, if we may judge by experience, their views of their interest are precisely the opposite."[11] He recognized the great challenge for any republic: "It requires the greatest wisdom and moderation to extend over any country a system of equal laws; and it is this very diversity of interests, which is found in all associations of men for a common purpose, that constitutes the main difficulty in forming and administering free and just governments." Unless some barrier be raised to preserve liberty for minorities, then majority rule will become "despotic power." Calhoun concluded: "The essence of liberty comprehends the idea of responsible power—that those who make and execute the laws should be controlled by those on whom they operate."[12]

As Calhoun reviewed the short history of the republic, he noted that the constitutional system provides, "on the side of the States, no means resorted to in order to protect their reserved rights against the encroachments of the General Government; while the latter has, from the beginning, adopted the most efficient to prevent the States from encroaching on those delegated to them."[13] That "most efficient" means was the U.S. Supreme Court, which had the "right of final interpretation" and thus "the power, in reality, of nullifying the acts of State Legislatures." But according to the common understanding of the constitutional system, this same Supreme Court also stood as the "only means" of protecting *states* from abuses of power by the federal government. Calhoun dismissed this interpretation as "a strange misconception of the nature of our system—and, in fact, of the nature of government." The problem was that giving the Supreme Court this ultimate power elevated one branch of the federal government "above the parties who created the constitutional compact" and "divest[ed] the people of the States of the sovereign authority."

Here Calhoun cited Jefferson's Kentucky Resolutions and Madison's Virginia Resolutions. He concluded with Madison and Jefferson that the states alone must "have the right of deciding on the infractions of their powers, and the proper remedy to be applied for correction." He added, "The right of judging in such cases is an essential attribute of sovereignty—of which the States cannot be divested without losing their sovereignty itself." Calhoun quoted directly from Jefferson's Kentucky Resolutions: "The Government, created by this compact, was not made the exclusive or final judge of the extent of the powers delegated to itself; since that would have made its discretion, and not the Constitution, the measure of its powers; but, as in all other cases of compact between parties having no common judge, each party has an equal right to judge for itself."[14]

Heretofore, Calhoun had raised no new constitutional interpretation or theory. He had simply reviewed and affirmed the Jeffersonian principles of limited government. Where he did push forward into new territory was in the development of Madison's concept of "interposition." Calhoun specified that the aggrieved state could exercise its right of interposition to veto any particular law or federal policy, not through action by its legislature but through a state constitutional convention. Indeed, he said that it was "not only the right of the State, but her duty, under the solemn sanction of an oath, to interpose, if no other remedy be applied."[15]

The South Carolina legislature's special committee

released the Exposition in December. The legislature passed and sent to Congress a formal protest against the tariff and simultaneously printed four thousand copies of the Exposition, though it stopped short of implementing Calhoun's interposition policy. The South looked desperately to the newly elected Jackson administration for relief.

In response to the nullification challenge, northerners foresaw sheer anarchy. Rhetoric intensified and positions solidified on both sides, while Calhoun desperately sought a middle ground that would protect the South but uphold the Union. He firmly believed that a state had the right to suspend a law within its own borders, yet he knew full well that no state could long remain in the Union in rebellion against the federal government. Along with Jefferson, he offered interposition or nullification as a temporary protest—a means of appeal. It allowed time for other states to weigh the charge of unconstitutionality, and if three-fourths of the states were so moved, they could amend the Constitution. Writing to his friend Duff Green, a newspaper editor, Calhoun laid out his position: "The ground we have taken is that the tariff is unconstitutional and must be repealed—that the rights of the South have been destroyed, and must be restored—that the Union is in danger, and must be saved."[16]

Duels

In January 1830 the debate burst onto the floor of the United States Senate. Daniel Webster of Massachusetts and Robert Y. Hayne of South Carolina engaged in verbal combat for several days before a packed gallery. As presiding officer of the Senate, Vice President Calhoun—the real spokesman for the South—gazed down on the duel in pained silence. Although an accomplished orator, Hayne was intellectually no match for Calhoun or Webster. He presented his case well, but he was careless with some of the more intricate details, affording Webster the opportunity for a strong rebuttal.

After capitalizing on Hayne's misstatements, Senator Webster launched a strong defense of the national government, grounded in the federal system, and concluded with one of the most memorable lines in American history: "Liberty and Union, now and forever, one and inseparable." As Calhoun gaveled the chamber to order, senators and spectators sensed that they had witnessed a debate of truly historic proportions.

The Webster-Hayne debate was quickly followed by another decisive event: a Jefferson Day dinner that Calhoun's supporters organized to bring pressure on the Jackson administration to lower the tariff. Washington's Indian Queen Hotel, the exterior of which was marked by a huge painting of Pocahontas, was the scene of the festivities on April 13, 1830. The room was packed with many southerners and Calhoun supporters from around the country. With Secretary of State Martin Van Buren at his side, President Jackson was seated across from Vice President Calhoun. Those in attendance noted that Jackson and Calhoun eyed each other furtively throughout the multicourse dinner. According to a newspaper account, the numerous toasts and speeches were of "a strong anti-tariff and rather of an anti-federal complexion," so much so that the Pennsylvania members "seceded and withdrew."[17]

Jackson and Van Buren, however, were determined to use this forum to squelch the growing divisions in their administration. The president had come to the affair armed with a succinct, trenchant toast. At the appropriate moment, the toastmaster dramatically announced, "The president of the

United States." Jackson slowly stood, raised his glass, and, as the cheers subsided, looked straight at Calhoun as he uttered these soon famous words: "Our Union—it must be preserved." A hush fell over the room, soon followed by nervous murmurings. All eyes turned to Calhoun as he slowly rose. Many noted that his hand seemed to shake as he raised his glass. With his eyes riveted on Jackson, he responded, "The Union, next to our liberty most dear."[18]

Word of the "dueling toasts" spread rapidly across the country. It was apparent to all: Jackson had failed to quell the rebellion, Calhoun had defiantly answered the challenge, and the battle lines had formed.

"The Last Great Effort to Save the Liberty of This Country"

Jackson's reelection campaign in 1832 brought the tariff issue to the fore. In November, just after Jackson secured reelection, South Carolina held a constitutional convention to protest the tariff. On November 24 the convention acted to nullify the tariffs of 1824 and 1828. Though not present at the convention, Calhoun wrote from his plantation, Fort Hill, hailing the action as "the last great effort to save the liberty of this country."[19] President Jackson responded with surprising conciliation in his annual address to Congress on December 4, but just six days later he issued his famous proclamation declaring nullification unconstitutional. He laid out his view that each state had surrendered part of its sovereignty upon entering the Union and that therefore neither nullification nor secession was an available constitutional option. Jackson was clear: "The laws of the United States must be executed.... Disunion by armed force is treason."[20] Two days later, on December 12, the South Carolina legislature volleyed back by electing Calhoun to the United States Senate. By month's end, Calhoun had resigned the vice presidency. Tensions rose around the country. Calhoun left Fort Hill for Washington, stopping in Columbia, Raleigh, and Richmond along his way to confer with the respective governors. He sensed that Jackson had overplayed his hand and advised his fellow southerners to advance with caution. While Virginia passed a more moderate resolution in support of South Carolina, and other southern states began to debate the issue, Kentucky's Henry Clay began frantically to seek a congressional compromise on the tariff. Calhoun signaled a willingness to compromise on any meaningful reduction to the tariff, but he adamantly opposed Jackson's Force Bill, which would grant special powers to the president to enforce the duties in South Carolina. A fierce debate between Calhoun and Webster ensued. Calhoun took to the Senate floor to denounce the Force Bill: "The bill violates the constitution, plainly and palpably, in many of its provisions, by authorizing the President, at his pleasure, to place the different ports of this Union on an unequal footing.... This bill proceeds on the ground that the entire sovereignty of this country belongs to the American people, as forming one great community, and regards the States as mere fractions, and not as integral parts of the Union."[21]

The result was compromise: Congress passed tariff reduction and also the Force Bill. Calhoun and his followers believed nullification had forced the reduction in the tariff, while Jackson and his followers believed passage of the Force Bill had ended the threat of nullification. Calhoun wrote shortly after, "Lying at the base of our political system and resting on truth and justice, it [nullification] is I trust and believe destined under Providence to arrest alarming growth of political corruption and to save the Constitution, the union and Liberty of these states."[22] Crisis was averted, for now. Years later Calhoun confided to friends, "If you should ask me the question what I would wish engraved on my tombstone, it is *Nullification.*"[23]

"Thinker and Prophet"

From 1816 until well into the 1850s, the tariff was the battleground issue of greatest national consequence. The Old Republicans saw the threat of executive tyranny in the successive battles to implement tariffs, banks, and internal improvements. Above all they feared an expanding federal government, which they knew would mean a bloated bureaucracy, patronage abuses by the executive branch, and the risk of ever higher tariffs. It was in these years of tariff warfare that Calhoun earned the sobriquet "the Cast-Iron Man." With relentless logic, unequaled intellect, and forceful personality, he became the revered spokesman, philosopher, and political leader of the South. At the same time, he earned the admiration of his opponents, Clay, Webster, the Whigs, and even the abolitionists. "The Cast-Iron Man" became a term of respect, even endearment.

Prior to the Nullification Crisis, Calhoun's public pronouncements and writings rarely mentioned slavery, but after 1833 he increasingly devoted his efforts to fighting both Jackson's expansion of the national government and the abolitionists' campaign against slavery and the South. Here we see Calhoun as the product of both his time and his region. He saw slavery as being at the very foundation of southern life, economics, and culture, and he found constitutional protection for slavery from the earliest days of the republic.

He discerned two closely intertwined dangers: the expanding federal government threatened the liberty of all the states and the Union itself, and this ever-encroaching government would be the means by which abolitionists would stamp out slavery and ruin the South. Ironically, Calhoun saw the preservation of slavery as critical to the preservation of liberty—and of the Union. He discarded Randolph's notion that slavery was a necessary evil and argued that slavery was a positive good. He remained dedicated to the preservation of the Union, which he believed was possible only if each state retained the power to nullify any action it deemed unconstitutional.

Because Calhoun's devotion to conservative principles became so identified with the defense of slavery and the ultimate dissolution of the Union, historians have too often ignored his considerable contributions to American constitutional history and conservative thought and his stature as one of America's greatest statesmen. His intellect was beyond dispute, and his honesty and consistency won the unqualified respect of his generation. On his death in 1850, Calhoun was widely eulogized throughout the South, as one would expect. But the comments of nonsoutherners, including abolitionists, were more revealing. William Lloyd Garrison lauded Calhoun: "He is a man who means what he says and who never blusters. He is no demagogue."[24] Wendell Phillips called Calhoun "the pure, manly and uncompromising advocate of slavery; the Hector of a Troy fated to fall."[25]

On the day following Calhoun's death, both Clay and Webster rose on the Senate floor to speak in tribute to their friend of so many years and so many legislative battles. Clay hailed Calhoun as "ever active, ardent, and able" and said "no one was in advance of him in advocating the cause of his country." He closed with these heartfelt words: "Sir, he is gone! No more shall we witness from yonder seat the flashes of that keen and penetrating eye of his, darting through this chamber. No more shall we behold that torrent of clear, concise, compact logic, poured out from his lips, which, if it did not always carry conviction to our judgment, commanded our great admiration. Those eyes and those lips are closed forever!...He possessed an elevated genius of the highest order...surpassed by no one....I was his senior, Mr. President, in years—in nothing else."[26]

Webster immediately followed Clay. He began by citing their thirty-seven years of friendship, which was always characterized by "a great degree of personal kindness." Although they differed on many questions, he said, "those differences never interrupted our personal and social intercourse." Webster praised Calhoun as a "man of undoubted genius and of commanding talent." He went on: "His mind was both perceptive and vigorous. It was clear, quick, and strong. The eloquence of Mr. Calhoun...was part of this intellectual character. It grew out of the qualities of his mind....His power consisted in the plainness of his propositions, in the closeness of his logic, and in the earnestness and energy of his manner." In closing, Webster added his personal assessment: "No man was more respectful to others; no man carried himself with greater decorum, no man with superior dignity....I have not, in public nor in private life, known a more assiduous person in the discharge of his appropriate duties."[27]

Two more recent evaluations of Calhoun were particularly insightful. On the unveiling of Calhoun's statue in Congress in 1910, Senator Henry Cabot Lodge of Massachusetts said:

> His statue is here of right. He was a really great man, one of the great figures of our history....There is no trace of the demagogue about him. He was a bold as well as a deep thinker, and he had to the full the courage of

his convictions.... He "raised his mind to truths." He believed that statesmanship must move on a high plane, and he could not conceive that mere money making and money spending were the highest objects of ambition in the lives of men or nations.[28]

Fifty years later, Calhoun's biographer wrote: "A statesman's value is relative, after all; and judged by later times, and his meaning for them. Calhoun stands in the first rank of men America has produced. *For as thinker and prophet, he was more important for later times than for his own* [emphasis in the original]."[29]

In the mid-twentieth century, Russell Kirk was among the first to recognize the lasting contributions of both Randolph and Calhoun to American conservative thought. He perceived something far deeper than a defense of slavery and a regional way of life. "Their arguments," Kirk wrote, "reveal how intricately linked are economic change, state policy, and the fragile tissue of social tranquility."[30] These statesmen employed their considerable gifts in defense of an ignoble cause, to be sure. Still, in articulating and advancing the "Old Republican" principles of limited government, the separation of powers, and liberty, they provided a philosophical foundation on which modern American conservatives have built.

4

GROVER CLEVELAND

Character and Courage

I naguration Day 1885 was "Restoration Day" for Jeffersonian conservatism. From 1800 until 1860, the Jeffersonians had generally dominated the federal government. Their party had vanquished the Federalists by 1816, and the Whigs, successors to the Federalists, never really established themselves as the dominant party. But by 1860 the Jeffersonian party—by then known as the Democratic Party—had splintered. Commencing with Abraham Lincoln's election that year, on the eve of the Civil War, a new party made up of former Whigs and Free Soilers, and calling itself the Republican Party, won six straight races for the White House. During this quarter century of Republican dominance, the federal government expanded at unprecedented rates.

Wartime demands always sanction governmental expansion

and threaten liberty, and those of the Civil War proved no exception. Governor Richard Yates of Illinois noted in 1865: "The war... has tended, more than any other event in the history of the country, to militate against the Jeffersonian ideal, that 'the best government is that which governs least.' The war has not only, of necessity, given more power to, but has led to a more intimate prevision of the government over every material interest of society."[1] The need for total wartime mobilization and the ensuing Reconstruction policies resulted in government intervention on a scale never before contemplated in America. The war was *the* defining event in the nation's history. Pulitzer Prize–winning historian James McPherson has described the effects of the Civil War: "The old decentralized federal republic became a new national polity that taxed the people directly, created an internal revenue bureau to collect these taxes, expanded the jurisdiction of federal courts, established a national currency and a national banking structure. The United States went to war in 1861 to preserve the Union; it emerged from war in 1865 having created a nation."[2]

As former Whigs, these Republicans not only waged a vast modern war but, at the same time, commenced the most massive public works project in human history—the building of the transcontinental railroad. The scale of this project far surpassed anything Henry Clay had dreamt of in his antebellum American System. The spanning of the continent by rail was accomplished with huge subsidies of land and financing from the government.

Having successfully fought the war and connected the two coasts by rail, the Republican Party now found itself astride a resurgent America and viewed itself as the legitimate protector and ruler of the Republic. The Republicans were now the self-proclaimed Grand Old Party (GOP), whereas the Democratic Party had been tainted as unpatriotic or pro-Southern.

The Jeffersonian notions of limited government, free trade, states' rights, and personal liberty seemed outdated.

The inevitable result of the exponential growth of government and the one-party rule during this twenty-four-year period was widespread corruption. Virtually all government appointees were political. Cronyism and conflicts of interest were rife. Time after time Congress expanded pension programs for veterans far beyond anything envisioned in the original 1862 veterans' bill. The protective tariff, which Republican Congresses repeatedly increased, became a method of rewarding and protecting various industries that had political influence. The historian Allan Nevins noted, "Ever since Appomattox the government had in great part been subject to the selfish materialism of the worst wing of the Republican party."[3]

But the Democratic Party gradually reemerged as a national alternative to the GOP. Horatio Seymour and Samuel J. Tilden, each of whom served as governor of New York, were old-line Jeffersonians who espoused limited government and opposed political corruption. They provided national leadership and were strong, but unsuccessful, presidential contenders in the 1868 and 1876 presidential elections, respectively. By the 1884 presidential election, a reform wing had emerged within the GOP. These "Mugwumps" called for the establishment of a civil service and an end to the rampant corruption and cronyism. It was from an alliance of Jeffersonian Democrats and Mugwumps that Grover Cleveland emerged on the national scene in 1884.

Cleveland's rise to the presidency was nothing short of meteoric. Born into a well-respected, well-educated, but financially straitened family in New Jersey, Cleveland did not attend college because of his family's financial difficulties. He settled in Buffalo, New York, where he became a respected, but hardly preeminent, lawyer. After serving a term as sheriff of Erie County, he was elected mayor of Buffalo in 1881 as a reform candidate. The relish with which he took on the corrupt political machines—both Democratic and Republican—brought him to the attention of the state Democratic Party, and in 1882 he was elected governor of New York. Once again, Cleveland took on corrupt machine politicians. He established his credentials as a strict constructionist by vetoing eight pork-barrel legislative acts in his first month in office. Within months he had earned the enduring enmity of both the Tammany Hall politicians, who were so active in the Democratic Party, and the Republican bosses.

When the GOP nominated former Speaker of the House James G. Blaine of Maine for president in the summer of 1884, the Democrats discerned a real opportunity for a long-sought presidential victory. Although an extremely able and attractive politician, Blaine was widely viewed as both personally ambitious and corrupt. The Mugwump faction of the GOP was thoroughly disenchanted by the prospect of Blaine's candidacy, and the Democrats believed the right reform candidate could siphon enough Mugwump votes to ensure a Democratic victory.

Samuel J. Tilden, the revered national leader of the Democratic Party, was the natural choice, but he declined to run because of age and ill health. The party frantically began sorting through the list of candidates, all of whom seemed to have detractors. At the Democratic convention, the New York delegation—the party's largest—put forward Cleveland as a favorite-son candidate. Already known for his government reform, Cleveland led on the first ballot but failed to secure the required two-thirds majority. On the second ballot, over the frenzied opposition of the Tammany Hall delegates, the convention swung decisively to Cleveland.

Having served for just one year as the mayor of Buffalo

and less than two years as the governor of New York, Grover Cleveland squared off against one of the most accomplished politicians of the age. The campaign was well remembered as among the bitterest in American history. Although Cleveland and Blaine refrained from personal attacks, their surrogates engaged in relentless mudslinging. Old allegations of Blaine's financial improprieties were recirculated. When it was revealed that Blaine had scrawled "burn this letter" across some implicating correspondence, the Democrats chanted, "Blaine, Blaine, James G. Blaine, the continental liar from the state of Maine, 'Burn this letter!'" Not to be outdone, the Republicans latched on to an old allegation that Cleveland had years earlier fathered an illegitimate child. Their chant became, "Ma, Ma, where's my Pa?" When confronted with the emerging scandal, Cleveland gave but one instruction: "Above all, tell the truth."[4] He admitted to paying child support and refused further comment.

For three days after Election Day, the vote was in doubt. Finally, when the votes were all counted, Cleveland was the victor. He had edged out Blaine by less than a quarter of 1 percent of the popular vote; the electoral vote was 219–182. The Democrats now had had a witty rejoinder to the Republicans' campaign slur: "Ma, Ma, where's my Pa? Gone to the White House, ha, ha, ha!" It is hardly a surprise that Cleveland told a friend shortly after entering office, "Sometimes I wake at night in the White House and rub my eyes and wonder if it is not all a dream."[5] Buffalo mayor to president in less than three years!

"Honesty, Courage, Firmness,
Independence, and Common Sense"

The American public had little idea what to expect from President-elect Cleveland, but it was not long before they knew. In the months between Election Day and the inauguration, he acted boldly on three defining issues: civil service reform, soundness of the currency, and the tariff.

On the first, he clearly signaled to his party, hungry for the spoils of victory, that all appointments would be based on merit and that no competent Republican would be summarily replaced. This pronouncement shocked much of the Democratic Party but confirmed for the reformers that they had backed the right man.

The question of silver coinage emerged unexpectedly in February 1885. In 1878 Congress had passed a law requiring the U.S. Treasury to purchase a certain amount of silver every month and convert it to silver dollars. Paper currency was redeemable in either gold or silver, and since the price of silver was lower than that of gold (and falling), more and more creditors demanded payment in gold. By February, this situation had depleted gold reserves, thereby undermining the soundness of the U.S. currency, which operated on the gold standard. Sound-money Democrats led by Tilden and Abraham Hewitt, chairman of the House Ways and Means Committee, implored Cleveland to support emergency legislation that would halt all silver coinage, which they believed would ensure the soundness of the currency. Over the strident opposition of many western and southern Democrats, Cleveland came down squarely for a sound currency. Allan Nevins, in his biography of Cleveland, concluded that this letter of support "served notice that Cleveland, following in the footsteps of Seymour and Tilden, would turn a face of granite against all inflationist schemes. By its very vigor it put heart into frightened bankers and restored confidence."[6]

The third matter on which President-elect Cleveland took a stand was the same one that Thomas Jefferson, James Madison, Nathaniel Macon, John Randolph, and John C. Calhoun had opposed so adamantly: the tariff. The tariff had become the federal government's primary source of funding. The Lincoln administration had introduced an income tax to finance the Civil War, but Congress repealed it in 1872. So in the years following, Republican Congresses repeatedly raised tariff levels over Democratic opposition. By the mid-1880s the tariff was producing sizable federal surpluses. The South and the West strongly opposed the tariff, however, and the Democrats' 1884 platform called for substantial tariff reduction. In the selection of his cabinet in early 1885, Cleveland showed that he would make good on that promise: every Cleveland nominee was a low-tariff Democrat.

With these early indicators of policy direction in place, Cleveland stood on the East Portico of the Capitol on March 4, 1885, and delivered his inaugural address in what was to become a trademark style of straightforward clarity. After a brief appeal for bipartisan cooperation, he turned to strict construction of the Constitution: "In the discharge of my official duty I shall endeavor to be guided by a just and unstrained construction of the Constitution, a careful observance of the distinction between the powers granted to the Federal Government and those reserved to the States or to the people, and by a cautious appreciation of those functions which by the Constitution and laws have been especially assigned to the executive branch."[7] The Old (Jeffersonian) Republicans could not have stated it more clearly.

From there, Cleveland laid out his views on economy in government. He spoke of economy in moral terms: "It is the duty of those serving the people to closely limit public expenditures to the actual needs of the Government economically administered, because this bounds the right of the Government to exact tribute from the earnings of labor or the property of the citizen, and because public extravagance begets extravagance among the people." To raise taxes from the public to cover expenditures in any amount beyond the most basic services amounted, in Cleveland's view, to extortion in the name of taxation. Furthermore, a profligate government would undermine the private virtue of thrift and destroy the very moral fiber of the citizenry. Cleveland exhorted the crowd, "We should never be ashamed of the simplicity and prudential economies which are best suited to the operation of a republican form of government and most compatible with the mission of the American people." He then warned government officials that they were selected to manage public affairs only "for a limited time" and were "still of the people," and that therefore through their example they should encourage "that plain way of life which among their fellow citizens aids integrity and promotes thrift and prosperity."[8] Again, Cleveland was taking a chapter directly from Macon and Randolph.

The new president next addressed the tariff question. He recognized the role of government in providing a sound economic structure to secure "the safety and confidence of business interests and make the wages of labor sure and steady." He pledged to "relieve the people of unnecessary taxation" and prevent "the accumulation of a surplus in the Treasury to tempt extravagance and waste."[9] Clearly, he intended to reduce the tariff.

Finally, Cleveland pledged honesty and genuine reform alongside the "application of business principles to public affairs."[10] As the crowd gazed on this rather ordinary-looking man and listened to his unembellished speech, many were not particularly impressed. He did not seem to exhibit extraordinary characteristics, and this impression was essentially correct. As Nevins concluded:

In Grover Cleveland the greatness lies in typical rather than unusual qualities. He had no endowments that thousands of men do not have. He possessed honesty, courage, firmness, independence, and common sense. But he possessed them in a degree that other men do not. His honesty was of the undeviating type which never compromised an inch; his courage was immense, rugged, unconquerable; his independence was elemental and self-assertive. Beneath all this was a virility or energy which enabled him to impose his qualities upon others in any crisis.[11]

Hence, the inaugural address was an accurate preview of what Cleveland was about to deliver. It would not be long before the American public knew that their new president was a man who said quite clearly what he meant, and he absolutely meant what he said.

"THE GOVERNMENT SHOULD NOT SUPPORT THE PEOPLE"

Implementing civil service reform consumed much of Cleveland's first six months in office. The sternness of his character became evident as he refused to award political patronage to his own party, despite the constant entreaties from Democrats. Within several months, leading Democratic newspapers were complaining of Cleveland's stunning lack of gratitude toward his fellow Democrats. He ignored the criticism and made it clear that the day of the political spoilsman was over.

Although it was twenty years after Appomattox, the Civil War still loomed large. "Pension fever" had infected

Congress, which sent the president bill after bill authorizing new payouts to veterans—pensions for veterans who had served only ninety days, for disabled veterans whose disability had nothing to do with their service, for veterans who had deserted, and so on. Cleveland believed the veterans' program had become a corruption-riddled federal welfare scheme that amounted to an outrageous raid on the Treasury. In the name of fairness and economy, he vetoed more than a hundred of these measures in the first year of his presidency. The politically savvy action for the first Democratic president since the Civil War would have been to avoid confrontation, express his patriotism, and sign the pension bills. But Cleveland had promised a government of economy, and he intended to deliver one.

In early 1887, Congress presented Cleveland with the so-called Texas Seed Bill, which brought sharply into focus the president's constitutional philosophy. This relatively minor incident provides valuable insight into Cleveland's principles and legacy, as well as the growth of government under subsequent progressive administrations. Several Texas counties had experienced a severe drought and were in dire need of seed grain. Congress sympathetically responded by passing a $10,000 grant for seed grain. Cleveland promptly vetoed the measure with a message that has been quoted by liberals, as evidence of conservatives' callous disregard for human suffering, and by conservatives, as evidence of strict constructionism. In rejecting the measure, the president said he could not approve a bill "to indulge a benevolent and charitable sentiment through the appropriation of public funds." He in no way denied the need for seed grain, but he said he could find "no warrant for such an appropriation in the Constitution." Cleveland also pointed out that the need could easily be met by charitable contributions. (In fact, some $150,000 in charitable contributions were quickly raised and dispatched to Texas.) Reminding Congress of the "friendliness and charity of our countrymen," he offered a prescient warning: "Federal aid in such cases encourages the expectation of paternal care on the part of the Government and weakens the sturdiness of our national character, while it prevents the indulgence among our people of that kindly sentiment and conduct which strengthen the bonds of common brotherhood."[12]

President Cleveland concluded with this memorable admonition, which is a classic statement of Jeffersonian conservatism: "A prevalent tendency to disregard the limited mission of this [the federal government's] power and duty should, I think, be steadfastly resisted, to the end that the lesson should constantly be enforced that, *though the people support the Government, the Government should not support the people*" (emphasis added).[13]

"Battling for an Honest Principle"

With the 1886–87 federal surplus topping $103 million, Cleveland turned his sights on tariff reduction. He believed these excessively high levels were enriching industrialists at the expense of consumers. Furthermore, in light of the surplus, the tariff rates represented a confiscatory level of taxation and tempted Congress to spend the surplus on various expansionary schemes.

To dramatize the issue, Cleveland devoted his third Annual Address to Congress entirely to the need for tariff reform. His message identified the economic burden borne by lower-class laborers and farmers while industrialists were being enriched under the pretense of economic protection. With vigor reminiscent of Calhoun some fifty years earlier, he denounced as both unjust and unconstitutional the favoritism in calling "our manufactures infant industries still needing the highest and greatest degree of favor and fostering care that can be wrung from Federal legislation."[14] Republicans opposed any reduction in the tariff, and many congressional Democrats preferred to retain the tariff to fund their own pork-barrel projects. If there was to be tariff reform, Cleveland would have to provide the leadership.

Throughout the congressional battle, Cleveland rallied Democrats behind reform, and he stubbornly refused to compromise with Republicans on the issue. With his reelection campaign on the horizon, Cleveland's political advisers urged him to compromise. His response was immediate and afforded an illuminating glimpse into his character: "What is the use of being elected or reelected, unless you stand for something?"[15]

After endless wrangling, a bill—substantially watered down from Cleveland's original proposal—passed the House, but it died a long, slow death in the Republican-controlled Senate. Disappointed but undeterred, Cleveland vowed to make tariff reform the major issue in his 1888 reelection campaign.

The Republicans quite willingly took up the challenge. They adopted a strongly pro-tariff platform and nominated the thoroughly reliable and morally upright governor of Indiana, Benjamin Harrison. Although a colorless, somewhat frigid individual, Harrison was both competent and honest—the anti-Blaine. The election was indeed fought out on the tariff issue, though it provided no clear mandate in the end. Cleveland's campaign was sadly mismanaged, whereas the Republicans mounted a well-funded, well-organized effort. Cleveland garnered a plurality of the popular vote but fell short in the Electoral College, 233–168.

Cleveland's response just days after the election was very much in character: "I don't regret it. It is better to be defeated battling for an honest principle than to win by cowardly subterfuge. Some of my friends say we ought to have gone before the country on the clean administration we have given. I differ with them. We were defeated, it is true, but the principles of tariff reform will surely win in the end."[16]

INTERREGNUM

There then ensued a four-year interregnum unique in American history. Cleveland reentered private life as senior partner in a major New York law firm while the Republicans eagerly reassumed power in Washington. Controlling the presidency and both houses of Congress, the GOP passed many measures to expand the scope and authority of the federal government, including the McKinley Tariff, which raised import duties yet again, and the Sherman Silver Purchase Act, which required the Treasury to purchase even greater amounts of silver (despite the depletion of gold reserves that had already occurred). Under the iron discipline of Speaker Thomas Reed (deferentially known as "Czar Reed"), Republicans cast aside Cleveland's conservatism and soon boasted of the first "billion-dollar Congress." From his vantage point in New York City, the former president saw little about which to boast.

After remaining respectfully silent for the first half of Harrison's administration, Cleveland reentered the fray on Jackson Day, January 8, 1891, with an address to Democrats in Philadelphia entitled "The Principles of True Democracy." It was one of his finest speeches and a clear articulation of his conservative philosophy. The themes were, predictably, strict constructionism, economy in government, sound currency, and tariff reform. He roundly denounced the McKinley Tariff as "an unjust tariff which banishes from many humble homes the comforts of life, in order that in the palaces of wealth luxury may more abound." Cleveland attacked the record of Czar Reed and the Billion-Dollar Congress as being far beyond the bounds of strict economy and a threat to basic American liberty. He concluded: "It is right that the influence of the Government should be known in every humble home as the guardian of frugal comfort and content, and a defense against unjust exactions.... It is right that efficiency and honesty in public service should not be sacrificed to partisan greed."[17] The first volley of the 1892 presidential election had been fired.

That same month, the silver issue reemerged. Just six months after passing the Sherman Silver Purchase Act, the Senate decisively passed a bill calling for the free coinage of silver—an inflationary policy that would remove any mandatory ratio of silver currency to gold and essentially take the United States off the gold standard. Free silver so appealed to southern and western Democrats that only one Senate Democrat voted against the bill. The sound-money Democrats, centered in the Northeast and led by Cleveland, were concerned about their party's direction and alarmed over the prospect of abandoning the gold standard. Many of Cleveland's advisers urged him to refrain from speaking out against free coinage. Several warned him that, if his private views were to become public, his political career would be destroyed. His response was predictable: "I am supposed to be a leader in my party. If any word of mine can check these dangerous fallacies, it is my duty to give that word, whatever the cost may be to me." When, in February 1891, the Reform Club of New York invited him to speak on the free silver issue, he responded with a strong letter in which he condemned "the dangerous and reckless experiment of free, unlimited, and independent silver coinage."[18]

Cleveland shrugged off the denunciations that came his way. He wrote to a friend, "At any rate, no one can now doubt where I stand."[19] Eastern Democrats rallied behind Cleveland, and even many southern Democrats seemed to pull back from the silver issue. As he prepared to campaign for president in 1892, he had staked out strong positions on the two most contentious issues of the day.

The fight for the Democratic nomination was fierce and bitter. It pitted East against West, conservatism against progressivism, strict constructionism against more flexible interpretation, economy against greater government spending. Cleveland's first presidential campaign had centered on an appeal for honesty, civil service reform, and efficiency; his second campaign had added tariff reform; and this third campaign combined the earlier appeals with a spirited defense of free-market capitalism and sound currency. Conservative eastern Democrats and reformers formed his base; his challenge was to hold southern Democrats against the western progressives. Aided by his Democratic opponents' lack of stature and by excellent campaign management (a change from four years earlier), Cleveland was renominated on the first ballot. The party had rallied behind him on the central issues of sound currency and tariff reform.

After James Blaine removed himself from consideration, the Republicans unenthusiastically renominated President Harrison on a pro-tariff platform. New York State would prove crucial in this election, as it had in Cleveland's previous races: he had carried the state in 1884 but lost it in 1888. In midcampaign, Tammany Hall forces sought to extract patronage promises from Cleveland in return for support in New York. In a tense meeting, Cleveland reportedly bellowed at the Tammany leaders: "Gentlemen, I will not go into the White House pledged to you or to anyone else. I will make no secret promises. I'll be damned if I will."²⁰ Cleveland then left the room, but his campaign managers were able to secure the reluctant support of Tammany without the benefit of the candidate's pledges.

As was the custom, the two candidates did little public speaking during the campaign. When President Harrison's wife died from tuberculosis in October, Cleveland respectfully suspended campaigning. Most pundits predicted a close outcome in the election, but Cleveland claimed the popular vote by a comfortable margin and won the Electoral College vote in a landslide, 277–145. Republicans—and Democrats—were shocked by the margin of victory. Cleveland appeared to have a mandate.

Soon, however, Democrats began besieging Cleveland for partisan appointments. Shortly before inauguration day, Cleveland confided to a friend: "I have a hungry party behind me and they say I am not grateful. Sometimes the pressure is most overwhelming, and a President cannot always get at the exact truth; but I want you to know that *I am trying to do what is right*" (emphasis added).²¹

"I Have Tried So Hard to Do Right"

In his second inaugural address, on March 4, 1893, Cleveland returned to his earlier themes. He led off with the silver issue: "Manifestly nothing is more vital to our supremacy as a nation and to the beneficent purposes of our Government than a sound and stable currency." He urged "prompt and conservative precaution" in guarding the soundness of the currency and preventing "depreciation in the purchasing power of the wages paid to toil."²²

Reflecting on the past four years of Republican rule and

the Billion-Dollar Congress, Cleveland cautioned, "The lessons of paternalism ought to be unlearned and the better lesson taught that while the people should patriotically and cheerfully support their Government, its functions do not include the support of the people." Economy in government was much on his mind as he spoke of it in moral terms similar to those employed in his 1885 speech: "The waste of public money is a crime against the citizen, and the contempt of our people for economy and frugality in their personal affairs deplorably saps the strength and sturdiness of our national character." In his first term, Cleveland had vetoed 414 bills, most of which were appropriations he deemed excessive; he would veto another 170 bills in his second term. His total of 584 vetoes still stands as a record for any eight-year presidency.

Turning to his own party, Cleveland spoke of the continuing need for civil service reform. He promised to make appointments based on competence and efficiency rather than "rewards of partisan activity" and to remove from government "the demoralizing madness for spoils."[23]

In conclusion, an earnest president recommitted himself to strict constructionism: "I shall to the best of my ability and within my sphere of duty preserve the Constitution by loyally protecting every grant of Federal power it contains, by defending all its restraints when attacked by impatience and restlessness, and by enforcing its limitations and reservations in favor of the States and the people." Unlike the crowd that gathered in 1885, those there in 1893 knew what to expect. Republicans and Democrats alike recognized Cleveland as an honest, forthright man who meant to deliver exactly what he promised.[24]

No sooner than he was inaugurated, a severe economic recession, now known as the Panic of 1893, struck. The stock market plummeted, unemployment rose sharply, bank failures became commonplace, and public confidence eroded. In times of economic uncertainty, Cleveland believed strongly that the primary role of government was to provide a sound currency in which the public could have confidence. To restore confidence, he advocated immediate repeal of the Sherman Silver Purchase Act and full restoration of the gold standard. In August he called a special session of Congress to repeal the act.

In the ensuing debate, a thirty-three-year-old Democratic congressman from Nebraska, William Jennings Bryan, harangued the House for three hours, pleading for the free coinage of silver. The House voted for repeal, 239–108, but the debate foreshadowed a coming schism in the Democratic Party. In the Senate, Democratic support for repeal was weaker. But Cleveland refused to compromise. He believed nothing short of repeal would stabilize the markets and restore confidence. On October 30 the Senate voted for repeal. The gold standard was restored, stability was restored to the markets, and the worst of the panic was over by the end of 1893.

In 1894 Cleveland turned again to tariff reform. The House passed the Wilson-Gorman Tariff Act, which greatly reduced the McKinley levies. In securing passage of these reductions, Cleveland reluctantly agreed to a 2 percent income tax on the top 10 percent of households (those earning more than $4,000 per year). When the legislation moved to the Senate, Republican special-interest groups removed most of the tariff reductions. An incensed President Cleveland protested that the resulting bill only slightly reduced the McKinley Tariff and fell far short of his campaign promise. This was one of the most painful defeats of his political career.

Although the Panic of 1893 was relatively short-lived, the U.S. economy endured a protracted recession that dominated Cleveland's second administration. Progressives in the Democratic Party became increasingly vocal in support of silver coinage and aggressive government intervention to aid various sectors of the ailing economy. Labor unrest added to Cleveland's problems, as he sought to maintain government neutrality between capital and labor. Within his own party, Cleveland retained the support of conservative eastern Democrats and the more conservative southern Democrats but lost the West and parts of the South. He completed his second term as an ideologically and politically isolated president. His sound-currency stand had split the Democratic Party, and his tariff-reform measures could not command enough bipartisan support to pass Congress. Indeed, in 1896 his party veered sharply away from him on both issues. At the Democratic convention that year, the party nominated Bryan on a free-silver platform in an outburst of frenzied emotion.

Cleveland viewed the nomination of Bryan as a betrayal of his policies and a disaster for his party. A faction of conservative Democrats bolted, backing a third party called the National Democratic Party. Although Cleveland gave his tacit approval to the splinter group, he refrained from any active role in the campaign. It was clear to all, however, that he was pleased when Bryan lost to Republican William McKinley, a man whom he respected and believed to be far more acceptable than Bryan.

Cleveland and his family retired to private life in Princeton, New Jersey, where he divided his time between active involvement in Princeton University affairs and his role as senior statesman in the Democratic Party. Until his death in 1908, Cleveland exerted his influence to advance conservative principles within the party. He was active in support of the conservative Alton Parker when the New Yorker secured the Democrats' 1904 presidential nomination, and he spoke out publicly with some frequency in these retirement years. His death in 1908 was met with genuine grief from the public.

Although he was by then seen as a spokesman from a bygone era, he elicited widespread appreciation for his character and integrity. It was reported that his last words were, "I have tried so hard to do right."[25] It was a fitting end.

From obscure beginnings, Grover Cleveland dominated national politics for the last quarter of the nineteenth century and wrote a significant chapter in the history of American conservatism. In some ways he was an ordinary man, but as Allan Nevins wrote, "He imposed himself upon his time in a way no mediocre man could for a moment have done."[26] As a reformer in a corrupt era, Cleveland breathed new life into the old Jeffersonian concepts of economy, limited government, strict constructionism, and personal liberty in the face of an ascendant, combative progressivism. In his unflinching devotion to these conservative principles he secured his place in the panoply of conservative heroes. But he will be equally remembered for his common sense, character, and courage.

5

CALVIN COOLIDGE AND ANDREW MELLON

Commonsense Government

On August 2, 1923, President Warren Harding died unexpectedly. Vice President Calvin Coolidge, vacationing at his father's farm in Vermont, was sleeping when word of Harding's death came by telegraph. His father called up to the second floor to deliver the news that President Harding was dead. Coolidge dressed, knelt by his bed to offer a short prayer, and then proceeded downstairs, saying, "I believe I can swing it."[1] He took the oath of office from his father, a notary, by the light of a kerosene lamp in the small family living room.

This was the first picture Americans got of their new president, and they liked what they saw. It is impossible to imagine a more appropriate backdrop for Coolidge's rise to the presidency. The product of rural America, he was a man totally without pretense—straightforward, frugal, and honest. Succeeding the popular Harding, Coolidge would prove a master at retaining the public's affection throughout his tenure as president and, indeed, throughout his life.

"Masterly Inaction"

By the election of 1920, the country had experienced nineteen years of progressivism under Theodore Roosevelt's Square Deal, William Howard Taft's conscientious enforcement of Roosevelt's reforms, and Woodrow Wilson's New Freedom. In addition to the domestic reforms, the massive effort required to wage World War I resulted in centralizing, interventionist policies. The advent of the United States as a world power brought the high-flown idealism of Wilson's Fourteen Points and the great fight over the League of Nations. The country was understandably tired from the war effort, but it also seemed exhausted by the exhortations of Roosevelt and Wilson for activism, reform, and government intervention. America was far removed indeed from Cleveland's conservative administration.

Republicans sensed the conservative swing in popular sentiment. The GOP's national convention brought a bruising contest for the party's presidential nomination. General Leonard Wood and Senator Hiram Johnson of California seemed like front-runners, but the convention was split. General Wood, the old Rough Rider, did not seem a good fit for a war-weary country, and the party regulars had never forgiven Senator Johnson for his role in Charles Evans Hughes's failure to carry California in 1916, which reelected Wilson. Another contender, Governor Frank Lowden of Illinois, the son-in-law of millionaire George Pullman, did not appeal to progressives, who viewed him as too conservative. As the convention reached a stalemate, the party bosses convened in a smoke-filled hotel room and settled on Ohio senator Warren Harding. Harding, who had spent five unremarkable years in the Senate, was decidedly a dark-horse candidate: he had drawn only about 6 percent of the vote on each of the convention's first five ballots. But he was an effective compromise candidate, since he did not alienate various constituencies the way the other contenders did. Just as important, he was a conservative in the mold of William McKinley, representing, in the words of historian Paul Johnson, "the 'old America' before the Wilson watershed."[2]

Harding, who had been a small-town Ohio newspaper editor before entering politics, projected just the sort of image and values the American people were looking for in 1920. He was congenial but dignified, conservative but not reactionary, formidable but not intimidating. He seemed just the right sort of man to return the country to "normalcy." As the historian Frederick Lewis Allen noted, "There might be no such word in the dictionary as *normalcy*, but normalcy was what they [the American people] wanted."[3] Even the progressives saw something appealing in Harding: the *New Republic* wrote, "Harding stands for a kind of candid and unpretentious reaction that anyone can respect, and that a great many people momentarily desire."[4]

Although the party bosses pushed Harding through, the Republican delegates rejected the bosses' choice for vice president. Instead they put forth Governor Calvin Coolidge of Massachusetts. Coolidge had been thrust onto the national stage in the summer of 1919 with the Boston police strike. This strike was set against the backdrop of the first Red Scare, as Americans recoiled from the excesses of the Russian revolution and feared the spread of bolshevism and anarchy. In addition, the labor reforms of the past twenty years were encouraging millions of Americans to strike in the postwar period. The Boston police strike received widespread national press coverage, particularly when the leading labor organizer of the day, Samuel Gompers, got involved. As negotiations between the police commissioner and Gompers intensified, Governor Coolidge sought to find a peaceful, nonconfrontational solution.

Coolidge responded with skill and deliberation to defuse the potentially explosive situation. He waited until the critical moment, when negotiations began to fall apart, to issue this terse but dramatic statement: "There is no right to strike against the public safety by anybody, anywhere, anytime."[5] The sound bite struck a chord with Americans. Public sentiment swung against the police officers who had left their duty to go on strike, and Coolidge became a national celebrity. In the words of biographer David Greenberg, "The pithy pronouncement was classic Coolidge, neatly articulating what struck many as commonsense wisdom with a tautness that made it ripe for repetition in newspapers, newsreels, and conversation."[6]

More significantly, this episode foreshadowed how Coolidge would govern as president. He tended to work intensely, but quietly, on a problem until he became convinced of the correct plan of action and that the time for action was at hand. Then he acted decisively. He was arguably better at carrying out Teddy Roosevelt's admonition "Speak softly and carry a big stick" than Roosevelt himself.

The Republican delegates in Chicago had accurately read the times in nominating Harding and Coolidge. The Republican ticket was elected in a landslide, taking more than 60 percent of the popular vote and 404 of the 531 electoral votes. The Republicans swept the congressional races: the GOP's Senate margin rose from two to twenty-two, and the party controlled nearly 70 percent of seats in the House of Representatives. Coolidge declared years later in his autobiography that the election of 1920 repudiated the progressivism that had "tinged our whole political and economic life" for the first two decades of the twentieth century. The election ended an era that had "seemed to substitute words for things."[7]

Harding exercised his electoral mandate by cutting government expenditures an astounding 40 percent from Wilson's postwar levels, decreasing taxes, promoting an environment conducive to capital deployment, and pursuing a mildly internationalist foreign policy. On the domestic front, Harding successfully dealt with the severe recession of 1920 by lowering government spending, cutting taxes, allowing wages to fall, and encouraging business investment to return. By late 1921 the economy was booming. As Paul Johnson has written, this was "the last time a major industrial power treated a recession by classic laissez-faire methods, allowing wages to fall to their natural level."[8] Harding was governing as an old-line Jeffersonian, much in the mold of Grover Cleveland.

Coolidge was comfortable with the conservative philosophy of his predecessor, but he brought a more systematic and focused philosophy of government to the office than did Harding. He was dedicated first and foremost to the rule of law. Coolidge began his political career in the waning days of Lord Salisbury's career and developed a philosophy of government similar to that of the British prime minister. Salisbury often compared the English nation to a boat being carried downriver, with the function of a wise government being "merely to put out an oar when there is any danger of its drifting into the bank." Paul Johnson has noted that Coolidge practiced a policy of "masterly inaction."[9] The historian Amity Shlaes agrees, writing in her Coolidge biography: "Most presidents place faith in action; the modern presidency is perpetual motion. Coolidge made virtue of inaction."[10]

Many contemporaries underestimated Coolidge as a politician and a president. They mistook his restraint and inaction for weakness. Coolidge realized: "The people know the difference between pretense and reality. They want to be told the truth. They want to be trusted. They want a chance to work out their own material and spiritual salvation. The people want a government of common sense."[11]

Walter Lippmann, a leading political commentator of the day, wrote perceptively during Coolidge's presidency: "Mr. Coolidge's genius for inactivity is developed to a very high point. It is far from being an indolent activity. It is a grim, determined, alert inactivity which keeps Mr. Coolidge occupied constantly."[12] A key to understanding Coolidge's philosophy of intentional inaction lies in the advice he once gave to Herbert Hoover: "If you see ten troubles coming down the road, you can be sure that nine will run into the ditch before they reach you, and you have to battle with only one of them."[13] Coolidge was consistently a minimalist, very much in line with Jefferson's and Madison's early writings on limited government and strict constructionism.

THE MELLON PLAN

As he settled into the presidency, Coolidge retained Harding's cabinet, which included Andrew W. Mellon of Pittsburgh as treasury secretary. Mellon was probably the second-richest man in American behind John D. Rockefeller and was widely seen as a financial genius. By profession a banker, Mellon had structured, financed, and controlled some of the great names in American industry, including Alcoa, Gulf Oil, Carborundum, and Koppers. His personal fortune was estimated to have been $300–400 million in the 1920s.

Mellon had long been active in Pennsylvania Republican politics, although he never ran for office. Shy and averse to publicity, Mellon avoided the limelight. In declining to give a commencement address in 1923, he explained that his few attempts at speechmaking had turned out to be "a painful ordeal."[14] A reporter commented that Mellon's gray flannel suit seemed to be the color "that most effectively describes his personality," and others discerned "a tired double-entry bookkeeper who was afraid of losing his job."[15] Though a major financial backer of the GOP, he was generally thought to be above partisan politics, and his appointment by Harding was widely applauded. By Harding's death, Mellon was generally regarded as the administration's leading cabinet member. On the floor of the House in 1922, a congressman labeled him "the greatest Secretary of the Treasury since Alexander Hamilton," much to Mellon's embarrassment.[16]

Secretary Mellon quickly became Coolidge's most trusted adviser. Coolidge brought to the partnership considerably more commitment than had Harding. Together Coolidge and Mellon developed and implemented the fiscal policies that provided the framework for the great economic expansion of the 1920s. A modern historian has written, "Between Coolidge and Mellon there was also a personal bond." Both were men of few words, and it would be said of them that "they conversed entirely in pauses."[17] Theirs was a shared faith in minimal government, individual responsibility, and free markets.

In 1924 Mellon published his various writings and proposals to Congress under the title *Taxation: The People's Business*. Known also as the Mellon Plan, the program featured four elements. First, he called for reducing the top income tax rate from 77 percent to 24 percent. He predicted that investors would pour their tax savings into equity investments, which would produce economic growth. Second, Mellon advocated cutting the lowest income tax rates from 4 percent to 0.5 percent to lower the burden on those "least able to bear it." Third, he sought significant reductions in the federal estate tax to encourage investment as opposed to tax evasion. Fourth, he said that the government "can and should be run on business principles," which included balancing the budget and reducing debt.[18]

Mellon articulated the philosophy behind his proposals: "Any man of energy and initiative in this country can get what he wants out of life. But when initiative is crippled by legislation or by a tax system which denies him the right to receive a reasonable share of his earnings, then he will no longer exert himself and the country will be deprived of the energy on which its continued greatness depends."[19] Coolidge stoutly endorsed Mellon's views, saying in his inaugural address, "The wise and correct course to follow in taxation and all other economic legislation is not to destroy those who have already secured success but to create conditions under which everyone will have a better chance to be successful."[20] Because tax rates affected the behavior of business and investors, Mellon and Coolidge argued, lower tax rates would produce general economic growth and also higher revenues for government. The Mellon Plan was a precursor of the Laffer Curve, which gained prominence under President Ronald Reagan.

Mellon so dominated fiscal policy debate throughout the twenties that it was quipped, "Three presidents [Harding, Coolidge, and Hoover] served under Mellon." In 1924 the progressive senator Robert La Follette, well known for his hyperbole, declared in a Pittsburgh speech: "Andrew W. Mellon is the real president of the United States. Calvin Coolidge is merely the man who occupies the White House."[21] As with much of La Follette's rhetoric, this claim was untrue. Theirs was a true partnership, with Coolidge providing the political support needed to advance Mellon's plan. The details of the treasury secretary's plan fit perfectly with Coolidge's philosophy of individual liberty and limited government. Coolidge used the presidency to articulate this vision, as he did in a speech in August 1924: "I want the people of America to be able to work less for the government and more for themselves. I want them to have the rewards of their own industry. This is the chief meaning of freedom. Until we can reestablish a condition under which the earnings of the people can be kept by the people, we are bound to suffer a very severe and distinct curtailment of our liberty."[22] Given his strong philosophical commitment to economy in government, it is no surprise that Coolidge championed Mellon's proposals more than Harding did. Mellon understood the importance of Coolidge's support, expressing his "confidence in the president's courage and political sense."[23]

In his first year as president, Coolidge spoke often about the need for cutting taxes. The federal income tax was only ten years old, but during the Great War, Congress had enacted huge increases on all levels of income. When the federal income tax was introduced in 1913, the highest bracket paid a tax of 7 percent; despite peace, the top bracket in 1920 paid a whopping 77 percent. When Harding entered office in 1921, the economy was in a steep recession. Secretary Mellon believed substantial tax reductions were needed to boost growth. The Revenue Act of 1921 achieved modest reductions, but now Coolidge and Mellon strongly urged Congress to return rates to their prewar levels. Congress and the president finally compromised with the passage of the Revenue Act of 1924, which reduced the top income tax rate to 40 percent.

Tax reductions were to become the centerpiece of Coolidge-Mellon economic policy. The public embraced tax reform, as Coolidge's resounding reelection in 1924 confirmed. Although largely ignored by most historians, the presidential election of 1924 is remarkable in several aspects. Much as the far more heralded election of 1912 represented the "high tide of progressivism," the 1924 election can be viewed as the "high tide of American conservatism." Among twentieth-century presidents, Coolidge was the most Jeffersonian in philosophy and practice; his opponent in 1924, John W. Davis, was the last nominee from the conservative, Jeffersonian wing of the Democratic Party. In retrospect, 1924 was a watershed election, as thereafter the GOP has been the more conservative party, while the Democrats have shifted ever more leftward. Franklin Roosevelt commented shortly after Election Day 1924 that it was useless for the Democrats "to wear the livery of the conservative"—a lesson the Democrats have not yet forgotten.[24]

"Economy and Taxation as Moral Issues"

Following the 1924 election, as a victorious Calvin Coolidge prepared to assume the presidency in his own right, he delivered three major addresses that were to define his administration.

On December 3 he sent his annual State of the Union message to Congress, and in it he renewed the call for lower taxation. Not content to settle for the compromise of the Revenue Act of 1924, Coolidge made it clear to Congress that he viewed his election victory as a mandate for lower taxes. He contended that "the larger incomes of the country would actually yield more revenue to the government if the basis of taxation were scientifically revised downward."[25] The *Washington Post* offered a summary of the State of the Union that could have applied to Coolidge's entire political career: "The concise, straightforward presentation of facts with regard to the state of the Union, the short simple sentences which can be understood without effort, and the common sense of the whole message combined to make a strong appeal." The message was received with bipartisan acclaim as the "best message Mr. Coolidge has sent to the Capitol."[26]

On January 17, 1925, he delivered the second of his major addresses before the American Society of Newspaper Editors. It was here that he uttered those famous, and much misunderstood, words, "The chief business of the American people is business." Coolidge had simply observed that Americans "are profoundly concerned with producing, buying, selling, investing, and prospering in the world." But he did not stop there. In fact, he declared that "the accumulation of wealth can not be justified as the chief end of existence," and he praised idealism and condemned materialism: "It is only those who do not understand our people, who believe our national life is entirely absorbed by material motives. We make no concealment of the fact that we want wealth, but there are many other things we want much more. We want peace and honor, and that charity which is so strong an element of all civilization. The chief ideal of the American people is idealism." His message was clear: prosperity is the result of the character of the American people, not the government. Historians, however, have too often lifted "The chief business of the American people is business" out of context and portrayed Coolidge as a tool of big business.[27]

In his third major speech, the inaugural address of March 4, 1925, Coolidge was widely praised for his comprehensiveness and brevity, "rarely equaled by the utterances of presidents," according to the *Washington Post*. Here again Coolidge preached that economy in government was a cardinal virtue:

The resources of this country are almost beyond computation. No mind can comprehend them. But the cost of our combined governments is likewise almost beyond definition. Not only those who are now making their tax returns, but those who meet the enhanced cost of existence in their monthly bills, know by hard experience what this great burden is and what it does.... *I favor the policy of economy, not because I wish to save money, but because I wish to save people.* The men and women of this country who toil are the ones who bear the cost of the Government. Every dollar that we carelessly waste means that their life will be so much the more meager. Every dollar that we prudently save means that their life will be so much the more abundant. *Economy is idealism in its most practical form* [emphasis added].[28]

Modern historians have generally failed to understand the moral dimension of Coolidge's philosophy and have instead viewed him as a mouthpiece for big business. But to Coolidge, the case for lowering taxes and reducing government spending went far beyond the need to run government as a business. To the president, it was immoral for the government to take one penny more from the taxpayer than was absolutely necessary to maintain law and order and provide the most basic services of government. The *Washington Post* captured the essence of Coolidge and his philosophy in this editorial comment on his address:

Few persons, probably, have considered economy and taxation as moral issues. But Mr. Coolidge so considers them, and his observations give a fresh impression of the intensity of his feeling on this subject. He holds that economy, in connection with tax reduction and tax reform, involves the principle of conservation of national resources. A nation that dissipates its resources falls into moral decay. Extravagance lengthens the hours and diminishes the rewards of labor. "I favor the policy of economy," says Mr. Coolidge, "not because I wish to save money, but because I wish to save people." He would protect those who toil by preventing the waste of the fruits of their toil. The burden of taxation is excessive. It makes life more meager, and falls hardest upon the poor. The United States is fortunate above other nations in the opportunity to economize. It is at peace and business activity has been restored. "The collection of any taxes which are not absolutely required, which do not beyond reasonable doubt contribute to the public welfare, is only a species of legalized larceny," is Mr. Coolidge's vigorously expressed conclusion on the subject of economy.[29]

After the modest reductions of the Revenue Acts of 1921 and 1924, in February 1926 Coolidge and Mellon achieved the comprehensive congressional victory they had long sought: the Revenue Act of 1926 was passed by overwhelming majorities in both houses of Congress. This sweeping legislation removed fully one-third of the 1925 taxpayers completely from the tax rolls, halved the estate tax, and repealed the gift tax. Progressives mounted fierce resistance in the Senate, characterizing the bill as tax relief for the rich. But the bill returned more than 70 percent of the tax reductions to taxpayers with incomes below $10,000 per year. Nebraska's Senator George Norris charged that Andrew Mellon's personal tax reduction was larger than the aggregate reduction of all the citizens of Nebraska. Secretary Mellon did not bother to rebut this charge, but historian Thomas Silver has retorted that "in

1924 Andrew Mellon paid *more* federal taxes than all the people of Nebraska put together."[30]

Reduced taxes and limited government interference fostered unprecedented economic growth through the 1920s. The gross national product grew at an astounding annual average rate of 4.7 percent; the unemployment rate declined from 6.7 percent to 3.2 percent; and consumer prices remained stable. People across all tax brackets benefited. Between 1922 and 1928, the number of taxpayers earning more than $100,000 quadrupled, and the average income reported by this bracket increased 15 percent. Similarly, the number of taxpayers in the $10,000 to $100,000 bracket increased 84 percent. The number in the lowest bracket, those earning below $10,000, actually declined. In the words of Paul Johnson, "Prosperity was more widely distributed in the America of the 1920s than had been possible in any community of this size before."[31] The tax reform also put an exemption on the first $4,000 of annual income. As a result, by 1928, *98 percent* of the population paid no income tax at all. Silver has concluded, "It is only a tiny exaggeration to say that Coolidge and Mellon completely removed the burden of federal income taxation from the backs of poor and working people between the time Coolidge entered the presidency and the time he left."[32]

Moreover, as Mellon and Coolidge had forecast, lowering tax rates actually increased the government's gross tax receipts substantially, creating annual surpluses and allowing for federal debt reduction. A modern economist has written: "The tax cuts of the 1920s were the first federal experiment with supply-side income tax rate cuts.... The Mellon tax cuts restored incentives to work, save, and invest, and discouraged the use of tax shelters."[33]

The Purpose of Government

One of Coolidge's greatest congressional struggles involved the McNary-Haugen Farm Relief Bill. Before and during the First World War, America's farm acreage and production exploded to meet international demand, and the price of farmland boomed. But after the war, farm prices collapsed and thousands went bankrupt across America's midwestern farm belt. The McNary-Haugen Bill arose in 1924 as an effort to help these farmers. The legislation proposed to have the federal government purchase domestic agricultural surpluses and sell them overseas, raising domestic farm prices. Eastern and southern opposition defeated the bill in June 1924, but the progressive farm bloc resurrected the bill in the following session of Congress. Proponents of McNary-Haugen picked up strength in the 1926 congressional elections and also won certain key Republican converts, including Vice President Charles G. Dawes and Agriculture Secretary Henry Wallace. Coolidge, supported strongly by Mellon, voiced opposition during the congressional debate, but the bill easily passed both Houses, only to be vetoed by Coolidge.

In his veto, the president forcefully characterized this legislation as a radical intrusion of the federal government into the free market. He gravely warned against granting "almost unlimited control of the agricultural industry" to a twelve-man board that could "not only fix the price which the producers shall receive for their goods, but can also fix the price which the consumers of the country shall pay for these commodities."[34]

In a Jeffersonian argument that other conservatives would articulate in opposing New Deal legislation in the 1930s, Coolidge decried the idea of "equalization": "This so-called equalization fee is not a tax for purposes of revenue in the accepted sense. It is a tax for the special benefit of particular groups."[35] Coolidge would continue to battle McNary-Haugen through the rest of the term. Congress again passed the bill in 1928, and again Coolidge wielded his veto.

On December 4, 1928, Coolidge sent his final State of the Union message to Congress, and the themes were familiar. The message understandably began with optimism: "No Congress of the United States ever assembled, on surveying the state of the Union, has met with a more pleasing prospect than that which appears at the present time." He extolled the importance of both tax and debt reduction and reviewed the usual issues relating to agriculture and the tariff. In closing, he sounded his final, oft-repeated call for conservative government:

> The end of government is to keep open the opportunity for a more abundant life. Peace and prosperity are not finalities; they are only methods. It is too easy under their influence for a nation to become selfish and degenerate. This test has come to the United States. Our country has been provided with resources with which it can enlarge its intellectual, moral, and spiritual life. The issue is in the hands of the people. Our faith in man and God is the justification for the belief in our continuing success.[36]

This was Coolidge's last official reminder to the public that the strength of the Republic lay in the people—not in the government. The government's primary role was to provide stability and opportunity for free individuals to excel.

"The Things That Are Unseen"

Throughout American history, conservatism has often been defined in juxtaposition to the incumbent government—or in opposition to government policies and expansion. Like Grover Cleveland before him, Coolidge actually achieved a record of substantial success in implementing conservative principles. His success was the result of unswerving perseverance and focus. In addition to having, in Secretary Mellon, an equally dedicated believer in economy, low taxes, and limited government—"commonsense government," as they called it—Coolidge was unrelenting in his drive to reduce government expenditures and taxes. Amity Shlaes has written, "As documented in White House appointment books, whereas other presidents met sporadically with budget advisers, Coolidge met faithfully and weekly with his Budget Bureau director, General Herbert Mayhew Lord."[37] Coolidge said near the end of his presidency: "I favor the American system of individual enterprise, and I am opposed to any general extension of government ownership and control. I believe not only in advocating economy in public expenditure, but in its practical application and actual accomplishment."[38] His conservative presidential successors have enjoyed considerably less success in implementing their principles.

The results of his perseverance were impressive. Government expenditures fell steadily: from 1921 through 1928, the federal budget was reduced by an astounding 35 percent. The federal debt was reduced, unemployment dropped as low as 3 percent, and the economy boomed. More Americans entered the middle class than ever before. In general, Coolidge was determined to pull government back and give Americans the opportunity to excel.

Beyond the impressiveness of his official record, there was an underlying integrity that bound together the private and the public Coolidge. The *Washington Post* was correct in observing that Coolidge spoke of his economic policies in moral terms. He devoutly believed in the sanctity of work, thrift, honesty, forthrightness, and lack of pretense, and he carried a lifelong fear of the effects of debt and sloth. Coolidge spoke a language learned in rural New England from his family. In one speech he said: "Success must depend on individual effort. It is our theory that the people make the Government, not that the Government makes the people. Unless there abides in them the spirit of industry and thrift, of sacrifice and self-denial, of courage and enterprise, and a belief in the reality of truth and justice, all the efforts of the Government will be in vain."[39]

The economic manifestations of commonsense government were important to Coolidge, but he found even greater significance in the spiritual virtues. He did not believe in the perfectibility of man. Instead he feared that under the benefits of peace and prosperity, "It is too easy to become selfish and degenerate."[40] Coolidge lectured the nation regularly on the importance of spiritual matters. One of his most direct and memorable exhortations came in a 1923 speech, when he was still vice president:

> We do not need more material development; we need more spiritual development. We do not need more intellectual power; we need more moral power. We do not need more knowledge; we need more character. We do not need more government; we need more culture. We do not need more law; we need more religion. We do not need more of the things that are seen; we need more of the things that are unseen.[41]

Remarkably, in a decade of rapid social change and modernization, his message resonated consistently with the public. He earned and retained their confidence, respect, and even affection. In 1928 he stood at the height of his popularity and could have stood for reelection, yet he quietly stepped down with these few words: "I do not choose to run for president in 1928."

Financier, Statesman

Whereas Coolidge decided to take his father's advice, "It's better to leave while they still want you to stay," Mellon stayed on at Treasury under President Herbert Hoover. Both Coolidge and Mellon had developed a decidedly unfavorable opinion of Hoover during Hoover's tenure as Coolidge's secretary of commerce. Coolidge regularly referred unflatteringly to Hoover as "Wonder Boy," and Mellon feared Hoover's tendency toward government intervention in the economy. Because of Mellon's stature and reputation, Hoover needed him and persuaded him to remain at Treasury.

But faced with the 1929 stock market crash and the ensuing Great Depression, Hoover chose to disregard much of his treasury secretary's advice. Mellon famously advised Hoover to "liquidate labor, liquidate stocks, liquidate farmers, liquidate real estate" to "purge the rottenness out of the system."[42] He viewed the speculation, stock market crash, and depression as predictable excesses in a free-market economy, which would correct itself more quickly and efficiently without government intervention. Hoover succumbed to his engineer's "desire to tinker" and ignored Mellon's counsel. A frustrated and disheartened Mellon agreed to leave the Treasury and to accept the ambassadorship to Great Britain in 1931, where he served until Hoover's presidency ended in 1933.

By 1930, Mellon had acquired one of the greatest art collections in history and began developing philanthropic plans to donate the collection as the foundation for the National

Gallery of Art. In addition to the collection, which was valued at $40 million, he gave a $10 million gift for construction. Congress formally accepted the gift in 1937, but not before Franklin Roosevelt's Justice Department subjected Mellon to a long and humiliating tax investigation. President Roosevelt detested Mellon both as a person and as the representative of all that Roosevelt distrusted in the free-market 1920s. The Justice Department investigated Mellon's personal tax returns but could not even secure a grand jury indictment. Mellon denied all charges, and a two-year civil trial completely exonerated him in 1937—but only after his death, in August of that year. Upon his death, Mellon was hailed as "one of the last of our statesmen-financiers."[43]

"A Man Who Really Did the Nation Some Service"

After four years of retirement, Calvin Coolidge died in early 1933. The newspapers were filled with tributes to him. The *New York Times* retold how, during the 1919 Boston police strike, his friends had warned him not to issue his famous declaration because they felt it would end his political career: "'Very likely,' he said; and signed it." The article chronicled how the nation had turned gratefully to him as "a man of the highest integrity and honesty" amid revelations of scandal during the Harding administration. Numerous remembrances mentioned his humor. "What is your hobby?" a woman asked him at a Washington dinner party. "Holding office," he said. To the society matron whose husband had bet her she would be unable to get Coolidge to speak more than three words, he responded, "You lose." In addition to lauding his personal qualities, the obituaries noted his career-long commitment to individual freedom, limited government, and reduced taxation. The *Times* eloquently summarized his service:

> All during his life he never changed his character or methods. He listened, he assimilated, and he waited until there appeared what seemed to be the soundest course. He did not try to make circumstances; but, when they appeared in the right configuration, he acted. Otherwise he waited. His distinguishing characteristic was his ability to wait in silence. At first it made him a subject of ridicule.... Eventually his silence was regarded as a heroic manifestation and became a legend.[44]

Coolidge was buried, appropriately, on a Saturday, avoiding any undue disruption to the weekday business and personal lives of the citizens of Northampton, Massachusetts. After a simple, dignified service at the Congregational Church, a funeral motorcade proceeded to Plymouth Notch, Vermont, for the president's burial. In a cold winter rain, the thirtieth president of the United States was returned to the rocky New England soil whence he came. A plain headstone bears simply his name, the dates, and the presidential seal.

Perhaps the most surprising source of praise for Coolidge came from H. L. Mencken, a cynic not known for praising anyone or anything. Mencken wrote perceptively of Coolidge, "If the day ever comes when Jefferson's warnings are heeded at last, and we reduce government to its simplest terms, it may very well happen that Cal's bones now resting inconspicuously in the Vermont granite will come to be revered as those of a man who really did the nation some service."[45] Mencken probably wrote those words with little expectation that such a day would ever come.

6

JOSIAH W. BAILEY

THE CONSERVATIVE MANIFESTO OF 1937

The political ramifications of the 1929 stock market crash and the ensuing Great Depression were devastating to conservatism in general and to both the Republican Party and the conservative faction within the Democratic Party. Liberal Democrat Franklin Delano Roosevelt crushed the incumbent, Herbert Hoover, in the 1932 election and then won even more decisively in 1936— indeed, FDR claimed the biggest landslide in American history as he took 523 of a possible 531 electoral votes. Democrats also dominated Congress: after the 1936 election, they controlled the House with 334 seats to 88 for the Republicans and the Senate, 76 to 16. With liberal Democrats controlling the federal government, the Roosevelt administration made government expansion the prescription for the country's every ill. A torrent of New Deal legislation poured forth from Congress.

Yet the Democratic Party still retained a conservative minority that adhered to Jefferson's ideals. This small band of conservative Democrats grew increasingly distrustful of FDR and his New Deal activism. In 1937 these Democrats, with support from a handful of conservative Republicans, formulated a document that came to be known as "The Conservative Manifesto." Though often viewed as a historical footnote, this manifesto was an important milestone in the history of American conservatism—clearly articulating the importance of free enterprise, limited government, and separation of powers.

Senator Josiah W. Bailey, Democrat of North Carolina, led the push for the Conservative Manifesto.

"Uphill and Up-stream"

Josiah Bailey was in every way a product of his native state. Born in Warrenton, North Carolina, into a devout Baptist family, he graduated from Wake Forest College in 1893 with distinction in Greek and English classics. Family financial hardship prevented his attending Johns Hopkins for graduate study, but his father, a well-respected Baptist minister, assisted him in securing the editorship of the *Biblical Recorder*, the official organ of the State Baptist Convention, in 1895. For the next twelve years he ran the *Recorder*, often taking political positions on public education, the disenfranchisement of black voters, prohibition, women's suffrage, and other critical issues. At the age of thirty-three he resigned his editorship to begin the study of law. He quickly became one of the twenty best-paid attorneys in the state and a force in Democratic politics.

In 1912 Bailey endorsed Woodrow Wilson and led his campaign in North Carolina. By 1914 he was widely acknowledged as the leader of the more liberal faction within the state Democratic Party and asserted unabashedly, "I am a progressive Democrat."[1] Under Wilson, Bailey was appointed collector of internal revenue for eastern North Carolina, where he served for eight years. With the 1920 Republican victory, Bailey returned to private practice in Raleigh but remained an important party leader, even running for governor (unsuccessfully) in 1924. He supported Al Smith for president in 1928, when many party leaders in North Carolina opted to sit out the election because of Smith's urban Catholicism.[2]

In 1930 Bailey challenged the venerable incumbent senator Furnifold M. Simmons, who had dominated North Carolina Democratic politics for more than thirty years. Although Bailey's challenge was initially seen as an exercise in futility, he was able to position himself as slightly more progressive than Simmons and considerably more energetic. Bailey scored a convincing victory over Simmons and entered the U.S. Senate at age fifty-six. In a letter to a friend, Bailey wrote: "I shall go to the Senate with no view to cultivating popularity, for I have never seen the man who could divine what is popular. I have gone uphill and up-stream these thirty years. I shall continue in the same direction."[3]

True to his Baptist upbringing, Bailey defined issues in moral terms of black and white—never shades of gray. It was not difficult to goad Bailey into righteous indignation over even the most minor issue, and he was sometimes referred to as "Holy Jo." One political foe labeled Bailey "superethical, superconstitutional, and supercilious."[4] On his arrival in the Senate, the liberal magazine *The Nation* characterized North Carolina's new senator as a "diligent scholar whose devotion to abstract principles of right and wrong, and specifically to righteousness in civil and political affairs, borders on fanaticism." The magazine continued: "He is a brilliant but painstaking student whose mind quickly cuts through to the heart of a thing, with a logic that is irrefutable, and a command of language probably unequalled by any other living North Carolinian."[5] These personal characteristics, coupled with his underlying philosophy of government, were to define Bailey's service in the Senate. His guiding principles were pure Jeffersonian philosophy: devotion to limited government, strict constructionism, individual liberty, and economy in government. His foundation was at once religious and political: "Being a Baptist, I am liberal, and believe in liberty. Being a Democrat, I am a liberal and believe in liberty. Once we abandon the voluntary principles, we run squarely into Communism.... There can be no half-way control."[6]

Like many other Democrats who served enthusiastically under Wilson, Bailey became increasingly conservative later in his career. It was not so much a conversion to conservatism as a gradual realization that Wilson's progressivism had begun to undermine basic Jeffersonian principles. As the Great Depression deepened under Hoover, Bailey called for balancing the budget through lower spending and lower taxation. As early as 1931, he foresaw the damage that government activism could do to the economy and the nation: "The danger in such a situation is that ill-informed and inconsiderate men will get into the leadership and bring to pass measures that will not only not accomplish the purpose desired, but will actually do lasting injury to all of us."[7] Although he accurately presaged the effects of the New Deal, Bailey supported FDR in 1932 and headed his presidential campaign in North Carolina, perhaps displaying more enthusiasm for the party platform than for the candidate himself.

That platform called for a balanced budget and reduced

government expenditure. By Inauguration Day 1933, however, FDR had jettisoned these conservative principles. With the much-heralded "Hundred Days," the new administration led frenetic legislative activism designed "to get the country moving," massively expanding federal intervention into the economic life of the nation. Bailey now saw battle lines forming between "the bureaucrats in Washington and the representatives of the people in Congress." True to his character, he responded defiantly: "I shall go straight forward for economy, regardless of this stimulated propaganda proceeding out of the bureaus at Washington for the purpose of frightening our people, and thereby bringing pressure on me."[8]

By early 1937, FDR's mastery of the federal government appeared complete. It was against this background of apparent invincibility that the president overreached both his constitutional boundaries and his political base. The result was a conservative congressional backlash of enduring importance.

Packing the Court

During his first term, Roosevelt had grown frustrated over the Supreme Court's rulings that found New Deal legislation unconstitutional. By a narrow 5–4 majority the court had invalidated the Agricultural Adjustment Act, the National Recovery Administration, and the Guffey Coal Act, and Roosevelt fumed at what he saw as the court's thwarting of the popular will. Flushed with his great 1936 electoral victory, he believed he could remove the court's stranglehold on his program. In February 1937, FDR proposed what came to be known as his "court-packing" scheme. Under the flimsiest of pretenses, Roosevelt would expand the court from nine justices to fifteen.

This presidential proposal did more to galvanize conservative opposition to the New Deal than any other single event. As a legal scholar, Bailey reacted with genuine outrage. On February 10 the *New York Times* lead article reported preliminary responses from the Senate, with eleven in favor and sixteen opposed. Bailey was quoted at length: "I am opposed to any attempt whatever to enlarge the number of justices. The judicial department has always been and must always be absolutely independent of the legislative and executive departments. Governments exist upon popular confidence, and confidence in the courts is fundamental."[9]

On February 13 Bailey delivered a powerful attack on the court proposal over national radio. In what Senator Harry Byrd would later call "one of the classics of American oratory," Bailey systematically dismissed FDR's reasons for the proposal and concluded with the stern warning that the Supreme Court and the Constitution are inseparably linked, and that "to weaken either is to weaken the foundations of our Republic; to destroy either is to destroy the Republic."[10]

In a lengthy letter to newspaper editor W. O. Saunders, which Saunders published under the title "The Hard Way," Bailey laid out a well-reasoned opposition to the plan. He called on Congress to heed the "voice of history which teaches me that second thoughts are more to be trusted than first thoughts; that reason is better than impulse; that the long view is better than the view of apparent immediate self-interest." He urged his colleagues to "study the measures and seek the right."[11] The letter was reprinted in newspapers throughout the country, and Bailey disseminated almost a million copies of the letter nationally in the month after FDR announced his plan. On June 20, at Colby College in Maine, Bailey received an honorary degree and delivered the commencement address. He used this forum to denounce the "attack on the Court—a blow against that process of democracy most essential to its existence, the constitutional check on executive and legislative power." He warned, "A subservient Congress means a dependent court, and the two together mean government by Presidential decree and without restraint."[12]

Other conservatives in the Senate joined Bailey in opposing the court plan. Foremost among these supporters were Bailey's closest personal friends and political allies, the senators from Virginia, Carter Glass and Harry Byrd. This triumvirate led the conservative coalition that coalesced in the New Deal years and was to have lasting importance in the history of American conservatism.

Carter Glass was as forceful, colorful, and controversial as Bailey. Standing barely five feet tall and weighing in at 140 pounds, the feisty Glass was widely known and respected for his sharp intellect and his even sharper tongue. A veteran member of the House of Representatives, he had served with distinction as secretary of the treasury under Woodrow Wilson and was hailed as the "Father of the Federal Reserve System." By the time of FDR's election in 1932, Glass was a senior statesman of the Democratic Party, on solid political footing in his native Virginia and in no way beholden to FDR and the national party.

Glass was arguably the first prominent senator to break with FDR and certainly the most virulent in his attacks. In July 1933, Glass wrote to a friend to protest FDR's bank holiday: "I think the President of the United States had no more authority to close or open a bank in the United States than had my stable boy.... It looks to me as if Hoover carried the country to the edge of the precipice and this administration is shoving it over as fast as it can. I predict the righteous failure of every damned project that these arbitrary little bureaucrats are vainly endeavoring to put into effect."[13] Glass opposed almost all of Roosevelt's major New Deal legislation. In 1936 he wrote in disgust: "Now is about as good a time as anybody could find to die, when the country is being taken to hell as fast as a lot of miseducated fools can get it there. Nevertheless, it would be interesting to live long enough to see the thing tumble so that nobody could long doubt the infinite folly of what has been done for the past three years."[14]

The third member of this leadership triumvirate, Harry Flood Byrd, was an altogether different personality—courtly, soft-spoken, and gracious. Byrd was, however, equally devoted to limited government, strict constructionism, and especially economy in government. As governor of Virginia in the 1920s, he presided over an administration that became a model of efficiency, economy, and honesty. His famous "Pay as You Go" policy became the defining principle in Virginia government for a generation after his term. Byrd controlled Virginia state politics for four decades, and the "Byrd Machine" produced a steady stream of capable, honest, conservative leaders who ran the state in close conformity with Senator Byrd's wishes. These three senators were worthy successors of the Old Republicans—the Tertium Quids—of the previous century.

As the Roosevelt administration formally submitted its Judicial Reform Bill to Congress, bipartisan opposition was building within the Senate. Glass broadcast a national radio message in May attacking the plan: "I am speaking from the depths of a soul filled with bitterness against a proposition which appears to me utterly destitute of a moral sensibility and without parallel since the foundation of the Republic." He condemned the bill as "the attempted rape of the Supreme Court."[15] In June the Senate Judiciary Committee, by a 10–8 vote, rejected FDR's bill as unconstitutional, while the Supreme Court unexpectedly changed course and ruled the National Labor Relations Act constitutional by a 5–4 vote. Sensing defeat in Congress, the president tried to secure a compromise. Senate Majority Leader Joseph Robinson brought an amended version of the bill to the floor on July 6 with a rousing speech demanding party loyalty.

Bailey found the amended bill to be as unconstitutional as the original and led the floor fight against it. When Bailey rose on the Senate floor to respond to Robinson, the chamber fell silent; in Robinson's own words, "That rare thing, a successful and convincing argument, was being made on the Senate floor." Recognizing that the tide had turned, Robinson left the Senate chamber in the midst of Bailey's speech to telephone the attorney general: "Bailey's in there and he's making a great speech.... He's impressing a lot of people, and I tell you I'm worried."[16] To defeat the bill, the opposition needed to convince three undecided senators; Bailey's speech secured the necessary votes. Vice President John Nance Garner tried to broker a compromise, but Bailey refused to concede on what he saw as a fundamental constitutional issue. Roosevelt was forced to abandon court reform.

Ten "Paramount Principles"

Another development in 1937 contributed to the congressional revolt that ultimately produced the Conservative Manifesto. Despite Congress's willingness to enact Roosevelt's far-reaching, free-spending economic policies from 1932 to 1936, the economic recovery remained weak. Then, in mid-1937, the economy dipped back into recession. Suddenly the press was filled with talk of the "Roosevelt Recession."

The administration appeared divided over how to proceed. Treasury Secretary Henry Morgenthau Jr. advised the president to advocate tax reform and government spending reduction to reassure business and promote investment. But Roosevelt's liberal advisers denounced a "conspiracy of big business" as the cause of the recession. FDR vacillated, and his hesitation, coupled with the realization that the New Deal's deficit spending and government expansion had not ended the Depression, emboldened the conservative faction in the Democratic Party.

Throughout the year, Bailey spoke out on the economic crisis. In a March speech that was broadcast nationally and reported in the *New York Times*, he warned of the dangers of "the unbalanced budget" and predicted a day of reckoning "when any government goes on spending for six years like yours and mine has without balancing the budget."[17] On November 2, in a speech to the Economic Council of Worcester, Massachusetts, Bailey again preached financial restraint: "If President Roosevelt means business, he can balance the budget. If he does not do so, the United States is in for a period of inflation. If the people will let us, we can reduce government expenditures. The present rate is nine billion dollars; the government can be run on three billions."[18]

In early December, Senator Byrd hosted an informal luncheon honoring Lewis W. Douglas, former budget director and outspoken critic of the New Deal. In addition to Byrd, Glass, and Bailey, another half-dozen conservative Senate Democrats and, significantly, two conservative Republican senators attended the luncheon. After Douglas's formal remarks, the discussion turned to the possibility of forming a pro-business, bipartisan coalition to counter the New Deal. The group agreed to reconvene and pursue this end. In subsequent sessions, the senators decided to draft a broad statement of principles behind which conservatives in both parties could stand. They aimed to secure signatures from a sizable number of senators—perhaps even a majority of the Senate. The group also agreed to proceed in strict secrecy until the completed statement could be presented with signatures. Bailey was selected as chief draftsman, with strong assistance and support from his friend and fellow Democrat Harry Byrd and from Republican Arthur Vandenberg.

Aside from the fight against the court reform, there had been little in the way of bipartisan coalition building. Bailey became the leader in this effort. Writing to a friend in November 1937, he described the situation: "It seems to me that we are now at the crossroads where it will be absolutely necessary either to turn further to the left and control practically all business and agriculture or some concession will have to be made so that the industries in the United States can look forward with some degree of certainty to an uninterrupted program."[19] Bailey saw the manifesto as an opportunity to bring cohesion to the conservative opposition: "There must be a definite rallying ground. We must have an end of this business of one man denouncing regimentation, another denouncing Congress, another denouncing the President, another protesting the tariff, and so on. On the other hand, we must have a constructive policy upon which the American people may concentrate their support."[20]

Bailey was an enthusiastic proponent of the bipartisan nature of this effort, but he soon discovered that many sympathetic senators were timid. Conservative Democrats were hesitant to take on the popular president, and some Republicans were concerned that a bipartisan conservative coalition might dampen the prospects for a resurgent GOP.

As Bailey and his core group began to seek signatures, the strict confidentiality was broken. Republican Charles McNary, the Senate minority leader, feared that the manifesto would damage Republican election prospects and leaked the plan to the press. On December 16 the *New York Times* broke the story with a front-page article. The following day both the *Times* and the *Washington Post* provided additional coverage. What had originally been termed "An Address to the People of the United States" soon became known as "The Conservative Manifesto." Its tone was well-reasoned, reflecting Bailey's authorship and none of Carter Glass's inflamed rhetoric. Though not explicitly anti-Roosevelt, it was stoutly conservative and aimed at appealing to a wide range of conservative senators; it was widely reported as an anti-administration plot, however.

The manifesto's preface addressed concerns over the recession and the need to abandon deficit spending and reaffirm basic free-market principles. The statement called for reliance on "liberal investment of private savings as a means of employment" rather than continued increases in public spending. "It ought to be borne in mind that private enterprise, properly fostered, carries the indispensable element of vigor."

The manifesto laid out ten points, or "paramount principles":

1. "The capital gains tax and the undistributed profits tax ought thoroughly to be revised at once...so as to free funds for investment."
2. Government spending must be reduced to achieve "a balanced national budget, and an end of those fears which deter investment."
3. The United States must bring an end to "coercion and violence in labor relations" and ensure "the constitutional guaranties of the rights of person and of property—the right of the worker to work, of the owner to possession, of every man to enjoy in peace the fruits of his labor."

4. "We oppose every government policy tending unnecessarily to compete with and discourage [private] enterprise."
5. "The value of investment, and the circulation of money, depends upon reasonable profit, not only to protect the investment and assure confidence, but also to provide increasing employment, and consumption of goods from farm and factory. We favor the competitive system as against either private or government monopoly."
6. "Credit depends upon security," and so policies must safeguard "the collateral which is the basis of credit."
7. "There ought to be a reduction in the tax burden, and if this is impossible, firm assurance of no further increase to be given."
8. "Except where State and local control are proven definitely inadequate, we favor the vigorous maintenance of States right of home rule and local self-government. Otherwise we shall create more problems than we solve."
9. "The administration of relief [to the unemployed, poor, and suffering] ought to be non-political and non-partisan, and temporary," as well as "economical," so as to encourage "individual self-reliance" and maintain "the natural impulses of kinship and benevolence of local responsibility in county, city, and state."
10. "We propose to preserve and rely upon the American system of private enterprise and initiative, and our American form of government. It is not necessary to claim perfection for them. On the record they are far superior to and infinitely to be preferred to any other so far devised. They carry the priceless content of liberty and the dignity of man."

The document concluded with these words: "Pledging ourselves to these principles, we summon our fellow citizens without regard to party to join with us in advancing them as the only hope of permanent recovery and further progress."[21]

Press coverage the following day focused on the leak and the resulting failure to secure senators' signatures. A *New York Times* editorial began, "Premature publicity, one of the most deadly of political diseases, seems to have overtaken the plan for a new conservative 'coalition' in the Senate." The editorial commended the principles as "all good points, on which emphasis at the present time is particularly appropriate," but predicted that the desired coalition would not materialize.[22] Similarly, the *Washington Post* encouraged Congress "to undertake the task of working out [an economic] recovery program of their own" but concluded that "a coalition between conservative Democrats and Republicans in the Senate is more interesting than factual."[23]

Having been prematurely exposed, the authors were not prepared to offer a consistent public defense of the measure. When the story first broke, only Bailey among the group of conservative planners acknowledged his part in drafting and defended the manifesto as "an affirmative policy." When, on December 20, Senator Edward R. Burke of Nebraska, a member of the conservative coalition, moved to have the manifesto inserted into the *Congressional Record*, Majority Leader Alben Barkley demanded to know the author. Bailey rose to defend the manifesto. Long considered one of the finest speakers in the Senate, he always drew a crowd, but on this occasion there was heightened interest. Vice President Garner left the rostrum and came to the Senate floor to hear Bailey. Supporters as well as opponents filed into the chamber for the speech. After reading the ten-point declaration, Bailey ended with this plea: "If there is a thing wrong in that statement, strike it out. If there is anything in it that offends you, condemn it. If you have a better paragraph, write it in. But, in God's name, do not do nothing while America drifts down to the inevitable gulf of collectivism.... Give enterprise a chance, and I will give you the guarantee of a happy and prosperous America."[24]

Bailey received a warm response on the Senate floor. Supporters, including Arthur Vandenberg and a number of other Republicans, gathered around him to offer congratulations. The business community responded favorably, too, with endorsements coming from *Business Week*, the *Wall Street Journal*, and the Chamber of Commerce. By February 1938, more than two million copies of the manifesto had gone into circulation.

Milestone

Bailey's vision of a bipartisan conservative coalition seemed for a brief moment a real possibility. With congratulations flowing in, the North Carolina senator was optimistic that FDR would respond to popular support and move to the right. He wrote hopefully to a friend in late December, "I may say to you that there are good evidences that the President wishes to turn decidedly to the right."[25]

Hope soon faded, however. Even as Bailey was writing that letter, the White House had convened a group of stalwart New Deal supporters to suppress the "conservative uprising." By early 1938 it had become clear that the early leak of the manifesto had eliminated any possibility of securing the forty-plus signatures Bailey had hoped for. The Senate had always been filled with men who were strongly independent in their views, and it was difficult for party leaders to exercise discipline among their members. But party loyalty made it even more difficult to bring cohesion across party lines. Although both the Democratic and Republican parties still supported conservative and liberal wings, the philosophical realignment of the parties that had begun with the 1924 presidential election had advanced by 1937. Ever since Franklin Roosevelt had warned Democrats that it was useless "to wear the livery of the conservative," the Democratic Party had moved to the left while the victorious Republicans held to the right. The realignment would continue in the coming decades, with progressive Republicans migrating into the Democratic Party and conservative Democrats (especially in the South) moving to the GOP. From a historical perspective, then, Bailey was ahead of his time in seeking a conservative coalition in 1937.

In that sense the manifesto was a watershed event, even if it would never serve the purpose Bailey intended for it. Conservatives agreed that the ten-point manifesto accurately expressed their foundational principles. The document offered clear evidence of congressional independence and resistance to New Deal assaults on Jeffersonian government, and it produced an identifiable bipartisan conservative bloc totaling some thirty senators.

That bloc would resist still more Roosevelt initiatives in the years ahead, for after vacillating between economic policies, FDR came down decisively in favor of accelerating government expansion and increasing deficit spending. The results were as Bailey had predicted. On May 9, 1939, a disheartened Treasury Secretary Henry Morgenthau reported to the House Ways and Means Committee: "I say after eight years of this Administration we have just as much unemployment as when we started. . . . We have tried spending money. We are spending more than we have ever spent before and it does not work."[26]

But under the leadership of Bailey, Byrd, and Vandenberg, the conservative voting bloc was able to restrain or defeat much New Deal legislation in the years leading up to World War II. In the postwar period, as we shall see in a later chapter, Senator Robert Taft provided the conservative leadership to form a powerful coalition of Republicans and southern Democrats that dominated Congress for more than two decades. The Conservative Manifesto of 1937 served as a rallying point for these conservatives, underlining the "paramount" importance of limited government, strict constructionism, separation of powers, and free enterprise.

"This I Have Done"

Josiah Bailey remained a respected leader of the Senate conservatives until his death on December 15, 1946. Upon Bailey's passing, his friend Harry Byrd issued the following statement: "In the death of Senator Bailey, the nation has lost one of its ablest and foremost statesmen. He was recognized by his colleagues as possessing the most brilliant and profound intellect in the Senate. His speech in 1937 in opposition to the packing of the Supreme Court will stand throughout the years as one of the classics of American oratory. I doubt if an abler speech was ever made in the Senate."[27] Former North Carolina senator Robert Reynolds, who had often opposed Bailey's conservatism, commented: "He considered his office a public trust and always did what he believed best for his people. He never used his office to promote his private interest."[28]

Bailey left an attachment to his will addressed to the people of North Carolina. Published some months after his death, the message identified three imminent dangers to the United States: (1) Soviet communism, (2) "ruthless" labor unions, and (3) reckless fiscal policies. Bailey concluded the section on the need for conservative fiscal policies by admitting, "There is absolutely no excuse for the extravagant civilian expenditure during the period in which I have been a Senator." He concluded the attachment with these simple words: "I shall always be grateful to the people of North Carolina for the great honor they gave me and the trust they reposed in me. It seemed to me from the outset that the least I could do by way of appreciation was to be honest with them. This I have done."[29] And so he had.

7

JOHN W. DAVIS

"Public Enemy Number One"

In his long career as a lawyer and statesman, John W. Davis received many sobriquets. During Davis's tenure as U.S. ambassador to the Court of St. James's, King George V labeled him "the most perfect gentleman." For many years as a leading Wall Street attorney, he was hailed as "the lawyer's lawyer." Newspaper reporters observing Davis's arguments before the Supreme Court said his was the "voice . . . of history itself." It is reasonable to speculate, however, that Davis's favorite was "Public Enemy Number One"—the name an agitated President Franklin Roosevelt and his New Deal supporters bestowed on him in 1935.[1]

Eleven years earlier, Davis had been the Democratic nominee for president. Now he led the resistance to the Democrats' New Deal, of which he said, "There has been no such bald challenge to the Constitution in American history." Davis saw an executive branch committed to government expansion and a compliant Congress unwilling to offer resistance. "If the structure of this Government is to be preserved," he said, "the courts must do it."[2] His success during the 1930s and 1940s in challenging before the Supreme Court the constitutionality of various New Deal laws provided an important chapter in the history of American conservatism.

"THE ABLEST MAN"

A native of Clarksburg, West Virginia, Davis was the son of John J. Davis, a U.S. congressman, prominent lawyer, and ardent Jeffersonian Democrat. The younger Davis reminisced in later life: "All his life my father was a pronounced individualist. I have never known any man who was more insistent on making up his own mind and really less inclined to yield to the opinions of others." Davis's mother, Anna, was reared and educated in Baltimore and brought both an active mind and a forceful personality to her marriage. Davis remembered his mother as "the most commanding person I ever knew."[3] She was a lifelong reader of the classics and, like her husband, a devotee of Thomas Jefferson. According to family lore, when Davis was born in 1873 (the first boy, after five daughters), Anna was engrossed in Gibbon's *Decline and Fall of the Roman Empire* late on the evening of April 13 but laid aside her reading to ensure that her son would be born on Jefferson's birthday.[4]

After receiving his primary and secondary education in Clarksburg, Davis completed his undergraduate college work at Washington and Lee University. In 1894 he entered the Washington and Lee School of Law, along with fifty fellow students under the two-man faculty of Dean John Randolph Tucker and Professor Charles A. Graves.

A commanding figure, Tucker was a former president of the American Bar Association and a former congressman. Davis later reflected that the dean's eloquent lectures "filled the dullest student with a perception of the majesty of the law."[5] Tucker was a passionate disciple of Jefferson and Calhoun and a devoted proponent of states' rights. He stood with Grover Cleveland against all forms of expanded government and for a stable, sound currency. These tenets of conservative thought took seed in young John Davis.

Professor Graves was, in Davis's opinion, "an educational genius." Much more professorial in style than Tucker, Graves was credited with grounding a generation of Washington and Lee students in the basics of common law. Davis revered Graves, saying, "I owe to him a debt beyond my power to repay."[6]

These two professors instilled in young Davis a respect for the law and a conservative worldview that would serve as his bedrock for his entire career. To Tucker, Davis owed his love of constitutional law; to Graves, his interest in real property. In later life, Davis approvingly recalled his legal training: "The professors were not so concerned with teaching us to criticize. They were more concerned that you should learn what the law *was*, than that you should be invited to speculate on what the law *ought* to be. I don't believe in educating the law student to be first a critic and afterwards a student. In law school, I don't think we students sat in judgment of the law."[7]

From W&L, Davis returned to practice law with his father, where he developed a statewide reputation as a skilled courtroom advocate, representing both corporate and individual clients. In 1910 Davis was put forward, against his father's and his own wishes, as the Democratic nominee for Congress. In a national Democratic sweep, Davis was elected from a traditionally Republican district and entered the House of Representatives in 1911. Reelected in 1912, he distinguished himself as a thoughtful, articulate member of the House Judiciary Committee and attracted the attention of President-elect Woodrow Wilson in 1913. Wilson appointed him solicitor general, a position Davis called "the most attractive office within the gift of the government for the man who loves the practice of law."[8]

Davis excelled in the position. His arguments were noted for their brevity, wit, and clarity. Within months of his arrival at the Supreme Court, every justice had expressed pleasure with his performance, according to Attorney General James Clark McReynolds. Justice Joseph Lamar admitted, "John W. Davis has such a perfect flow of language that we don't ask questions when we should." Observing Davis's impact on the court, one commentator compared the justices to "doting grandfathers enjoying the performance of a precocious and favorite grandson." The observer went on: "The Court fairly hovered over Mr. Davis in its solicitude, particularly Chief Justice [Edward Douglass] White. The Court can be most unapproachable and aloof in its demeanor toward the bar.... But it never heckled its fair-haired boy: John W. Davis."[9] The generally chilly Justice Charles Evans Hughes admitted it was "an intellectual treat" to hear Davis present an argument. Chief Justice White once remarked admiringly, "Of course, no one has due process of law when Mr. Davis is on the other side." Even the Supreme Court pages spoke of Davis's dignity, kindness, and graciousness. One page noted, "Everyone was rooting for Mr. Davis."[10]

Two successive chief justices, White and William Howard Taft, expressed their hope that Davis would be appointed their successor. On January 5, 1920, Davis made a revealing entry in his diary: "Sent off new year letter to Chief Justice White.

I shall always think that the greatest direct compliment I ever received was his statement when I went to say goodbye to him in Washington in December, 1918, that he had hoped that I might succeed him as Chief Justice. No man wants the bed in which he has slept narrowed to fit his successor."[11]

Davis's associates viewed him with a certain amount of reverence. Huston Thompson observed: "He never made an enemy I know of. I never heard him criticize a man." Robert Szold wrote: "Nobody could have treated me better. He was witty, pleasant, and unfailingly courteous. He always had time for small, kindly things." Above all else, said John Lord O'Brian, "John W. Davis had the gift of graciousness." They were agreed in their respect for Davis's grasp of the law and the power of his reasoning. "Everything was on a high level—his preparation, his oral argument, his personal relations," said Szold. "The whole atmosphere was of lofty dedication to the public welfare."[12]

Davis brought to the solicitor generalship a conviction that the proper role of the state was limited narrowly to the maintenance of order and national security and to the protection of private property and personal liberty. In 1915 Davis wrote to his father: "Human rights and rights of property are not different or antagonistic but parts of one and the same thing going to make up the bundle of rights which constitute American liberty. History furnishes no instance where the right of man to acquire and hold property has been taken away without the complete destruction of liberty in all its forms."[13] He further defined the government's role as ensuring that no group received preferential treatment—hence his positions on the tariff and antitrust.

As a Jeffersonian Democrat, Davis sometimes found it difficult to argue for his client, the federal government. There is no evidence that Davis's conservative views changed during his years as solicitor general. If anything, the opportunity to test and hone his views enabled him to move forward with an even more clearly defined conservatism. Davis argued more cases before the Supreme Court than any other solicitor general in history—before or since. He established a national reputation during this period, especially among lawyers and Democratic Party leaders, many of whom were also lawyers.

In 1918 Wilson appointed Davis ambassador to the Court of St. James's, where he served for two years in postwar London with real distinction. He returned to the United States in 1921 "dead broke" (in his own words) because of the significant personal expenditures demanded of a U.S. ambassador in those days—he had spent some $75,000 over and above his government salary. Davis joined Stetson, Jennings, and Russell, a major New York law firm, as senior partner. Interestingly, Grover Cleveland had been a senior partner at Stetson in the four years between his two administrations. Soon elected president of the American Bar Association, Davis served as lead counsel to J. P. Morgan and Company, AT&T, International Paper, and other major corporations. In 1922 he rejected an overture from Chief Justice Taft and the Harding administration to be nominated to the Supreme Court. Davis recognized that a lawyer could receive no higher honor, but he said that there was more "fun" on the bar's side, and in any case, he still needed to rebuild his savings.

Davis surfaced briefly as a dark-horse candidate for the 1920 Democratic presidential nomination. Four years later, the Democratic convention deadlocked between the two front-runners, Al Smith and William G. McAdoo. Finally, after three weeks and 103 ballots in ninety-degree heat (with no air conditioning), a bitterly divided Democratic Party nominated Davis as the compromise candidate. Walter Lippmann wrote, "They [the Democrats] acted on an intuition that told them that in an extreme crisis only the ablest man is good enough.... For they turned to the one candidate who embodied preeminently those very qualities for lack of which the party had almost destroyed itself."[14]

As the Democrats' nominee, Davis faced the impossible task of binding up his party's wounds while battling a popular incumbent in a booming economy. He waged a creditable campaign but still lost in a landslide to Calvin Coolidge and the GOP. As we have seen, this election marked the high tide of American conservatism—the last time both parties nominated conservative candidates.

"The Road to Socialism"

Soon after the 1924 election, Davis was back in his Wall Street office directing his growing firm, which had been renamed Davis, Polk, and Wardwell. He had never seen himself as a politician and fully understood that "the man who is out of politics more effectively than any other is a defeated presidential candidate." So he did not seek to play an active leadership role in the Democratic Party.[15]

Instead he provided counsel as an elder statesman. Davis testified frequently before congressional committees on the constitutionality of domestic measures and the advisability of foreign policy efforts. In 1929 he gave the Stafford Little Lectures at Princeton, which were published under the title *Party Government in the United States* and in which he explained the Jeffersonian concepts that underlay both the historic Democratic Party and his own political philosophy. Here he identified the "profound and lasting" struggle between paternalism and individualism—or "between the conservative and the liberal view of government and society." In words that foreshadowed his denunciation of the New Deal, he warned against paternalistic government that offered "a transcendental faith in the power and wisdom of the State and the human agencies it must employ." According to such a faith, he said, "in laws and still more laws lies the cure for every human ill, and fallible men when inducted into office are presumed to receive a mystic baptism of unselfish wisdom that fits them to administer the most intimate of their neighbors' affairs."[16]

In 1928 Davis gave quiet support to Democratic nominee Al Smith and spoke out forcefully against the religious bigotry aimed at the Catholic candidate. Following Smith's defeat and the onset of the Great Depression, Davis sought more actively to guide the party's direction as it approached the 1932 election. Davis went to the 1932 convention in Chicago as a delegate-at-large, hoping to nominate a conservative candidate. He received a rousing ovation when he spoke to the convention, and he helped persuade the party to adopt a relatively conservative platform. But he was not successful in securing the nomination for either Newton D. Baker or Harry F. Byrd, his two favorite conservative candidates. For some time Davis had believed that Franklin D. Roosevelt was too unpredictable to make a good president, even warning, "If that man is elected, he will ruin the United States."[17] Nonetheless, Davis announced his support for the ticket and attempted to hold the party to the conservative platform adopted at the convention.

Unlike many subsequent historians, Davis recognized the philosophical difference between President Herbert Hoover and his two predecessors. Harding and Coolidge were essentially Jeffersonians who advocated minimal government intervention; Hoover was far more of an interventionist. When Walter Lippmann posited that Hoover had been the forerunner of the New Deal, Davis wrote to Lippmann to express his complete agreement. Davis condemned Hoover's administration for following "the road to socialism at a rate never equaled in time of peace by any of its predecessors." He went on:

> I think that Hoover did make an unprecedented departure when he assumed that the national government is charged with the responsibility of the successful operation of the country's economics and the maintenance of a satisfactory standard of life for all classes in the nation. I do not believe that doctrine myself, first in point of right and second in point of power and capacity. Nothing but mischief, to my way of thinking, can come from any government attempting tasks which lie beyond its power to accomplish.[18]

In supporting Roosevelt in 1932, Davis did so on conservative grounds, in opposition to Hoover's interventionism. On October 30, 1932, a week and a half before the election, he wrote an article in the *New York Times* entitled "Why I Am a Democrat." In it he made the case for Roosevelt by harkening back to the party's Jeffersonian principles:

> Any nation that continues to spend more than it receives is headed for inevitable disaster; neither a nation nor a man can find solvency by borrowing; neither he nor it can spend its way into prosperity nor beg itself into comfort.... If the Democratic Party is successful, it will balance the budget.... Instead of striving to give every man a share of governmental help, borrowing from impoverished Peter to pay poverty-stricken Paul, it will aim to make it possible for every man to help himself.[19]

Davis's eloquent campaign appeal was soon to be replaced by his profound disillusionment with the New Deal.

"The Bounds Which Cannot Be Exceeded"

After Roosevelt's landslide election, Davis challenged the incoming administration to adhere to the party's Jeffersonian ideals. On March 5, 1933, as FDR took the reins of government, Davis wrote a major article in the Sunday *New York Times* entitled "The Torch Democracy Keeps Alight—Jefferson's Inspiration, Says John W. Davis, Is Still the Beacon of the Past." As clearly as any conservative Democrat has ever written, Davis laid out the Jeffersonian precepts of government:

> The chief aim of all government is to preserve the freedom of the citizen. His control over his person, his property, his movements, his business, his desires should be restrained only so far as the public welfare imperatively demands. The world is in more danger of being governed too much than too little.
>
> It is the teaching of all history that liberty can only be preserved in small areas. Local self government is, therefore, indispensable to liberty. A centralized and distant bureaucracy is the worst of all tyranny. Taxation can justly be levied for no purpose other than to provide revenue for the support of the government. To tax one person, class or section to provide revenue for the benefit of another is none the less robbery because done under the form of law and called taxation.[20]

Davis's worst fears were soon realized as FDR ignored the party platform and embarked on a course of government interventionism that made Hoover's policies look modest. In 1934 Davis complained that "the administration has moved away from me rather than I from the administration."[21] In August of that year he took the most active political position of his post-1924 career.

Along with other prominent conservatives of both parties, Davis founded the American Liberty League to defend Jeffersonian principles. He served for a time as executive director and headed the Lawyers' Committee. In soliciting financial support for the league, Davis outlined his personal philosophy:

> I believe in the Constitution of the United States; I believe in the division of powers it makes.... I believe in the right of private property, the sanctity and binding power of contracts; the duty of self-help. I am opposed to confiscatory taxation, wasteful expenditure, socialized industry and a planned economy controlled and directed by government functionaries. I believe these things to be inimical to human liberty and destructive of American ideals.[22]

Davis saw the Liberty League as a nonpartisan, educational institution that would expose the dangers of the New Deal and convince the public of the merit of Jeffersonian principles. He viewed with alarm the speed with which FDR and Congress were centralizing government and intervening in the economic affairs of the nation, warning that "those who stand for the old order must make themselves heard or the day will come when it will be too late for protest to be heard, much less followed."[23]

During the formation of the Liberty League, Davis delivered a major address at the University of Virginia—

appropriately, "Mr. Jefferson's University"—in July 1934. Warmly introduced by his old friend Senator Carter Glass, Davis condemned governmental attempts to undermine capitalism, decried economic planning, underscored the sanctity of property rights, pled for a return to greater individual freedom, and concluded with a plea for constitutional restraint:

> Every government of whatever kind professes always to be acting only for the public good. The bloodiest tyrants in history claimed no less. The limitations which our Constitutions seek to impose, however, are not intended to prevent Government and its agents from doing those things which no one could wish to do on any pretext, but rather to fix the bounds which cannot be exceeded even by conscious rectitude and righteous people. If these bounds can be over passed at will by the mere magic of the grand, omnific word "emergency," surely they are made of gossamer.[24]

Davis did not fail to appreciate the urgency of the Great Depression, but he saw as far more important the danger to the foundation of the American republic. His concern was that the New Deal "cure" was far worse than the disease. The growth of government intervention in the decades since—often justified as a response to an "emergency"—has demonstrated the wisdom of his words.

The Liberty League took the fight into the courts. Under Davis's direction, the Lawyers' Committee studied the constitutionality of the myriad New Deal laws and challenged those laws it believed were unconstitutional. In several instances, Davis appeared as an amicus curiae before the Supreme Court in attempting to thwart the Roosevelt administration. In the first of these cases, 1934's *United States v. Butler*, Davis offered a stirring defense of federalism and persuaded the court to invalidate the first Agricultural Adjustment Act, which he termed "a bribe to farmers."[25]

In 1935 Davis agreed to challenge the Frazier-Lemke Act in *Louisville v. Radford*. Passed in 1933, this act provided radical debt and bankruptcy relief for farmers through unprecedented government intrusion. FDR signed the bill despite the misgivings of many New Dealers. Davis saw it as an example of Roosevelt's willingness to experiment beyond the bounds of the Constitution. When the Fourth Circuit Court of Appeals upheld the act, Davis led the appeal to the Supreme Court. He argued that the act "does not deal with any subject over which power is delegated to Congress, and is, therefore, in contravention of the Tenth Amendment." In a sweeping reversal of the lower court opinion, Justice Louis Brandeis delivered a unanimous decision holding the Frazier-Lemke Act unconstitutional. Not surprisingly, Davis declared the court's ruling "a damn good opinion."[26]

That victory was soon followed by the fight over the Public Utility Holding Company Act of 1935. This measure promised centralized government control of the utility industry under the Securities and Exchange Commission. As a test case, the Edison Electric Institute sought out a bondholder in a bankrupt utility company and urged him to hire Davis in hope of securing a constitutional ruling before the act went into effect. Davis firmly believed that this act was unconstitutional and agreed to argue the case before a federal district court. Davis argued for more than two hours that the act violated the Constitution's Commerce and Due Process Clauses and charged that "no more pernicious doctrine was ever hatched or promulgated in the lives of this great free people." The court ruled decisively in Davis's favor, reciting much of his argument in its ruling. In a more limited ruling, the Fourth

Circuit Court of Appeals upheld the lower court, and the Supreme Court refused to hear the case. It was at this point that Harold Ickes, one of Roosevelt's most loyal henchmen, blasted Davis as a "vestal virgin guardian of the Constitution," and FDR labeled Davis "Public Enemy Number One."[27]

"A Great and Cancerous Bureaucracy"

In addition to these highly visible court challenges, Davis brought popular pressure against the Roosevelt administration. In December 1934 the American Bar Association broadcast nationally a fifteen-minute address in which Davis demonstrated his constitutionalism as well as his social and economic conservatism. He said:

> The Government set up for us at Washington is not and was never intended to be an eleemosynary institution or a foundation for miscellaneous charities. It was not designed as a universal parent or an earthly Providence.... I do not know of any shelter whatever in the fundamental law of the land, written or unwritten, express or implied, for many of the activities in which the Federal Government is now engaged.[28]

In early 1936 Davis made headlines in an address to the New York State Bar Association. He roundly condemned public officials' failure to defend the Constitution, and he specifically warned Congress that it was being reduced to the level of the Parlement of Paris in the eighteenth century, merely "registering the edicts of the king." He blamed the government—not business—for the lingering Depression: "A great and cancerous bureaucracy is no substitute for private judgment and initiative nor a cure for its mistakes."[29] He denounced the fatalism that saw centralization and collectivism as inevitable.

On February 5, 1937, Roosevelt submitted his court-packing bill to Congress, and Davis immediately took up the fight. He drafted an opposition statement, secured signatures of other prominent attorneys, and published it in major newspapers. He served as counsel to the group of senators, spearheaded by Josiah W. Bailey, who led the floor fight in Congress. Davis wrote a series of memoranda addressing the proposal's unconstitutionality; he distributed the memos to various senators and to political commentators, including Walter Lippmann. It was with great satisfaction that Davis saw the court-packing bill die in committee in late 1937.

Davis's victories over the New Deal before the Supreme Court and the defeat in Congress of the court-packing plan marked the turning points in FDR's domestic program. From 1938 on, Roosevelt was increasingly preoccupied by foreign affairs. The recession of 1938 laid bare the administration's claim of economic revival and gave conservatives in Congress leverage to block additional New Deal legislation. Davis supported FDR's foreign policy while keeping a watchful eye on the government expansion that inevitably accompanies war.

"The Greatest"

Between 1913 and 1954, Davis argued 140 cases before the Supreme Court. At his death in 1955, no other twentieth-century lawyer had equaled his record, and in American history, only Daniel Webster had exceeded it. The last two of Davis's cases before the Supreme Court provided a fitting conclusion to his appellate career.

The first of these was *Youngstown Sheet and Tube Co. v.*

Sawyer, known as the Steel Seizure Case. In 1952 the United Steel Workers of America threatened to strike. With the United States embroiled in the Korean War, President Harry Truman sought a way to prevent the strike. Truman refused to invoke emergency provisions of the Taft-Hartley Act, which governed the activities of labor unions. When he received his attorney general's opinion that he could, in case of emergency, seize the steel mills, Republic Steel sought Davis's counsel. In a detailed, eleven-page opinion, Davis responded that the president did not have constitutional authority to take control of the steel industry to avert a strike, even in wartime. Months later Truman announced the seizure in a divisive radio address that failed to bring the steel company executives into submission, leading to a legal showdown. The Supreme Court agreed to hear the case almost immediately. Davis had not been involved since delivering his opinion to Republic Steel, but at this point the industry's battery of lawyers asked him to argue their case before the court. The assignment was testament to the reverence in which his peers held Davis, then seventy-nine.

If ever there was the perfect confluence of events and the man, it was this case and John W. Davis. Convinced for the past twenty years that the government was dangerously overreaching its constitutional bounds, Davis had become the appellate champion of constitutional restraint. On May 12, clad in his traditional formal morning suit, he rose to make his argument before the Supreme Court. A reporter for the *New York Herald Tribune* wrote that Davis seemed "to personify the spirit of constitutionalism, his voice that of history itself."[30] Over the next eighty-seven minutes a packed courtroom was treated to a flawless performance by the greatest legal advocate in modern American history. Davis declared Truman's seizure not only a "usurpation of power without parallel in American history" but also a "reassertion of kingly prerogative, the struggle against which illumines all the pages of Anglo-Saxon history."[31] He drew repeatedly on the Jeffersonian principles he learned first from his father and later from Tucker and Graves at Washington and Lee. He concluded with Jefferson's own words: "In questions of power, then, let no more be heard of confidence in man, but bind him down from mischief by the chains of the Constitution."[32]

Many of the next morning's papers displayed a photograph of Davis striding confidently across the plaza of the Supreme Court. The eminent judge Learned Hand reported that he and his wife were finishing breakfast when she held up a copy of the *Herald Tribune*'s picture of Davis and said, "There, now that's the picture of a *really* distinguished man." Hundreds of congratulatory messages flooded Davis's office. But the greatest tribute was the Supreme Court's 6–3 ruling that the steel seizure had been unconstitutional.[33]

Davis's final argument before the court came in *Briggs v. Elliott*, the South Carolina companion case to *Brown v. Board of Education of Topeka*. This case involved the appeal of a ruling that upheld the constitutionality of segregation in South Carolina. Governor James Byrnes of South Carolina, a longtime friend of Davis's, asked Davis to take the case. The celebrated attorney agreed. This was not because Davis harbored special devotion to segregation. In fact, as solicitor general he had twice argued before the Supreme Court in defense of voting rights for black Americans, and had won both cases. And when he ran for president in 1924, he had forcefully attacked the Ku Klux Klan, declaring that the Klan—or any other organization that "raises the standard of racial and religious prejudices"—"does violence to the spirit of American institutions and must be condemned by all those who believe, as I do, in American ideals."[34] He took this principled stand despite the fact that his own Democratic Party drew major support from the Klan and was pressuring him to remain silent. By contrast, his Republican opponent, Calvin Coolidge, remained silent on the Klan issue.

But Davis saw *Briggs v. Elliott* as a clear-cut matter of stare decisis and states' rights. He was confident that the Supreme Court would uphold the highly esteemed Judge John Parker's lower court opinion, which rested squarely on precedent. Davis wrote to Byrnes that he did not believe the Fourteenth Amendment removed control of education from the states, and he concluded that the Supreme Court had already decided this very question in at least three previous cases.

Davis and South Carolina had precedent on their side, while the opposition relied on social science, morality, and appeals to conscience. When opposing counsel Thurgood Marshall submitted a brief filled with comments by sociologists, Davis expressed exasperation: "I can only say that if that sort of 'fluff' can move any court, God save the state!"[35] For Davis and many other conservatives, segregation—at least in the courts—was not a moral or sociological issue but a constitutional issue. Marshall and the civil rights advocates viewed segregation through an entirely different prism.

The pairing of Davis and Marshall was historic in itself. The seventy-nine-year-old WASP, a pillar of the establishment, was pitted against the forty-five-year-old black civil rights advocate, who later became a Supreme Court justice. Marshall spoke admiringly of Davis as "the greatest solicitor general we ever had." He added: "You and I will never see a better one. He was a great advocate, the greatest." As a law student at Howard, Marshall often slipped over to the Supreme Court to hear Davis argue cases. "Every time John Davis argued, I'd ask myself, 'Will I ever, ever...?' And every time I had to answer, 'No, never.'"[36]

More than three hundred people packed the Supreme

Court chamber on December 9, 1952, as Chief Justice Fred Vinson convened the hearing. The hopes of millions of black Americans and the fears of millions of white southerners were focused on the court as Davis and Marshall made their arguments. Several days after the trial, Davis wrote, "Unless the Supreme Court wants to make the law over, they must rule for me."[37] Immediately after the arguments, when the justices first met to discuss the case, there appeared to be a 5–4 majority in favor of upholding segregation. By spring, however, the court had turned 6–3 against upholding it. At this point the court asked for a reargument on five questions.

By December 7, 1953, when the reargument was held, a new chief justice, Earl Warren, had been installed. Warren was eager to put his stamp on the court and, perhaps, to atone for his role as governor of California in the internment of Japanese-Americans during the war. Again, the duel between Davis and Marshall was intense. *Time* described Davis, now past his eightieth birthday, as "a white-maned, majestic figure in immaculate morning attire who looks type-cast for the part." The magazine's report continued:

> Some of his friends were sorry to hear him, at twilight, singing segregation's old unsweet song. But the popularity of a case rarely cuts any ice with John W. Davis. In the 29 years since his defeat for the presidency, Davis has all but faded from popular memory; in his own profession, he is a living legend. Most Davis Polk business never reaches a courtroom at all. But the courtroom is still the showcase of the legal profession, and John W. Davis the acknowledged star of the show.[38]

Davis warned the court against sitting "as a glorified board of education" and appealed to the law's reverence for precedent. As Yale law professor and constitutional scholar Alexander Bickel has noted, "No one hearing Davis emphasize how pervasive and how solidly founded the present order was could fail to be sensitive to the difficulties encountered in uprooting it."[39] Again, Davis was certain that the court would uphold his argument, which relied on the most basic principles of Anglo-Saxon law. But on May 17, 1954, Chief Justice Warren produced a unanimous opinion that ruled segregation unconstitutional under the Fourteenth Amendment. Warren had done a masterful job of crafting a short, decisive opinion, overcoming the objections of several justices who were inclined to dissent until the final discussions.

Davis was devastated by the opinion—again, not because he was devoted to segregation but rather because he foresaw the danger that would come as the Supreme Court loosened those "chains of the Constitution" that Jefferson saw as the necessary restraint on government. In the *Briggs* ruling, Davis discerned what later conservatives would decry as "judicial activism." He observed to one of his partners that the opinion was "simply unworthy of the Supreme Court of the United States."[40]

Remaining active until the end, Davis died on March 24, 1955, in Charleston, South Carolina, during his annual winter visit to Yeamans Hall Club. The major newspapers hailed his remarkable career, civility, intelligence, and statesmanship. Walter Lippmann recalled of Davis: "I have seen a good many men under the awful temptation of the presidency. I have never seen another who had such absolute respect."[41] Shortly before his death, a reporter asked Davis what advice he might offer. He thought for a moment and, with a twinkle in his eye, said, "Let every man make an honest man of himself; then he can be sure there will be one less rascal." Good advice, indeed.

8

ROBERT A. TAFT

"Mr. Republican"

With the election of Robert Alphonso Taft to the United States Senate in 1938, the Republican Party began a revival as the conservative party in America. The GOP had sustained drubbings in 1932, 1934, and 1936 at the hands of Franklin Roosevelt and his New Deal Democrats. The low point came in 1936, when FDR won reelection in a historic landslide and congressional Republicans were annihilated. Only sixteen shell-shocked Republican senators survived, and they were timidly led by Charles McNary and philosophically divided. As we have seen, conservative Democrats led the first congressional resistance to the New Deal, in 1937.

It was onto this demoralized field of conservatives that Taft stepped in 1938.

"The Arbitrary Power of a Dictatorship"

As *Time* once observed, American politicians like to boast about "coming up from nothing," but Bob Taft "came up from plenty."[1] Taft's paternal grandfather, Alphonso, graduated Phi Beta Kappa from Yale in 1833 and transplanted the family from New England to Cincinnati, Ohio. There he established a leading law practice, invested wisely, and became a leading Ohio Republican. In the scandal-ridden administration of Ulysses S. Grant, Alphonso Taft served with distinction and without hint of corruption as secretary of war and attorney general. He later was appointed U.S. ambassador to Austria-Hungary. His five sons all graduated from Yale, all practiced law, and all were stout Republicans. A middle son, William Howard Taft, served as solicitor general, commissioner to the Philippines, secretary of war, president of the United States, and chief justice of the United States.

Will Taft's eldest son, Robert Alphonso, was very much the product of this family tradition. After dividing his childhood between Washington and the Philippines during his father's various tours of duty, he entered the Taft School, a New England boarding school founded by his uncle Horace. He graduated first in his class at Taft, proceeded on to Yale, where he again graduated first in his class, and studied law at Harvard, where he yet again graduated first in his class. At Yale he was a member of the secret society Skull and Bones, as were his father and grandfather. At Harvard he was editor of the *Law Review*. In 1910, when reporters asked the twenty-one-year-old Bob Taft what it was like to bear such a famous name, he responded: "I know it's an asset. It supplies the impetus which gives a man his start, but this impetus does not last forever. After the start, it is only by his own efforts that a man can keep going, and one with a family name has a lot to live up to."² From an early age, he was recognized within his remarkable family for his keen intelligence, independence, and relentless work ethic. Upon graduation from Harvard Law School in 1913, he declined, with characteristic independence, the offer to clerk for Supreme Court justice Oliver Wendell Holmes. He was anxious to return to Cincinnati and establish himself. He admitted years later, "I had a deathly fear that I would be accepted because of my father and not for myself."³ For the next twenty-five years, except for two brief stints in public service (at the Food and Drug Administration in Washington in 1917 and the American Relief Administration in Paris in 1918–19), Taft practiced law very successfully in Cincinnati while establishing himself as a leading figure in Ohio Republican politics, serving a term in the state senate. He turned down several opportunities to run for Congress and seemed quite content to focus on his growing family, his law practice, and Ohio politics.

For Taft, as for his whole generation, the defining event in the development of his political philosophy was the Great Depression. Always a serious student, Taft carefully analyzed what was wrong with the economy and brooded over the New Deal remedies. His analysis reinforced his conservative principles. Roosevelt's New Deal gave Taft "a concrete object against which to refashion core Republican principles," wrote Russell Kirk and James McClellan. "For Taft, the New Deal was an administrative mechanism to usher totalitarian or collectivist government into America."⁴

In 1935 Taft wrote:

> The New Deal is absolutely contrary to the whole American Theory on which the country was founded, and which has actually made it the most prosperous country in the world. It is inconsistent with democratic

government.... Communism, Fascism, Hitlerism have destroyed a system like ours in many European countries, and substituted a form of despotic socialism.... There is no man and no group of men intelligent enough to coordinate and control the infinitely numerous and complex problems involved in the production, consumption, and daily lives of one hundred and twenty million individualistic and educated people.[5]

As Taft's alarm over the New Deal increased, he simultaneously observed the paralyzed state of the Republican Party. The Democratic victories of the 1930s had caused philosophical waffling, confusion, and timidity within the GOP. At the 1936 Republican National Convention, Taft urged his party to "tell the American people that they cannot enjoy fancy government improvements and socialistic experiments without paying for them in increased taxation," and to return to the truth that "thrift, industry, and intelligence produce happiness as they produced it in the horse and buggy days."[6]

During the 1936 presidential campaign, Taft spoke often around Ohio on behalf of Alf Landon, the GOP nominee. Taft's two recurring themes were strict constructionism and federalism. He abhorred the experimental nature of the New Deal, the reliance on bureaucratic fiat as opposed to congressional statute. He believed Roosevelt's advisers saw the Depression as a convenient emergency by which any governmental action might be justified, regardless of constitutional limits. Their economic policies consistently promoted centralization of power in the national government at the expense of state and local government and the free market. Taft believed such concentration of power would not work and would erode personal liberty. On the campaign trail, he regularly warned: "History shows that once power is granted it is impossible for the people to get it back. In Greece republics gave way to tyrannies. The Roman Republic became an Empire. Medieval republics became monarchies. If we extend Federal power indefinitely, if we concentrate power over the courts and congress in the executive, it will not be long before we have an American Fascism."[7]

The GOP's disastrous electoral results in 1936 further convinced Taft of the need for conservative national leadership. He believed Landon's unwillingness to articulate core conservative principles and to confront the New Deal directly had contributed to his defeat.

In 1938 Taft decided to challenge incumbent Democratic senator Robert J. Bulkley. From the outset it was clear that Taft intended to campaign on sharply articulated conservative principles. As would be his practice throughout his career, he wrote his own speeches. Though never considered a gifted orator, he displayed a straightforward approach that conveyed a mastery of the issues. He was determined to make the New Deal the central issue: "I say that the regulation of wages, hours, and prices and practices in every industry is something which is, in effect, socialism; which is government regulation of the worst sort which means a totalitarian state. You cannot regulate prices in one industry unless you go on to others.... You can't carry it out without the arbitrary power of a dictatorship of some kind."[8]

Taft proved to be a relentless campaigner—but in his own way. He was hopelessly inept at small talk and at what H. L. Mencken termed "the art of boob-bumping," but he was able to communicate to the voters his earnestness, honesty, and intelligence. He spoke more than six hundred times in all of Ohio's eighty-eight counties. Senator Bulkley foolishly agreed to a series of three debates, after which it was widely conceded that Taft had scored a knockout with his mastery of facts, figures, and the issues. On Election Day 1938, Taft won with an impressive 54 percent of the vote. *Time* analyzed his election: "When Robert Alphonso Taft, 50, of Cincinnati, Ohio, has run for office, the electorate has done two things: 1) scoff at him, 2) vote for him. Mr. Taft is no charmer, but he gets elected."[9]

"Applying Old Principles to New Conditions"

Taft immediately became a national conservative spokesman. His unusual prominence as a freshman senator led to his being part of an ambitious series of national debates with a veteran Democratic congressman from Illinois, T. V. Smith. The transcript of these debates was published as *Foundations of Democracy* and provided a thorough summary of Taft's principles at the outset of his Senate career. He extolled the importance of equality of opportunity, as distinguished from any equality of outcome. He warned of the danger of high corporate taxes, which would "destroy all the incentive and initiative through which our success has been created." He continued: "Small business is the key to progress in the United States. It is a constant feeding of new men into business, which can only occur if small businessmen are successful, which develops new industries, and builds up more employment." In general, he urged, "The entire government policy of hostility to private industry should be abandoned." To resolve "the farm problem," he prescribed "a complete restoration of the market," noting that "limitation of production never has been successful in permanently increasing farm prices." He advocated that all welfare programs be designed, administered, and implemented on the state and local levels, with "federal grants conditioned on a proper non-partisan basis." Centermost in his philosophy was individual liberty:

> It is somewhat significant that the right endowed [in the Declaration of Independence] is not one of happiness but merely of pursuit.... The whole history of America reveals a system based on individual opportunity, individual initiative, individual freedom to earn one's living in one's own way, and to conduct manufacturing, commerce, agriculture, or other business; on rugged individualism, if you please, which it has become so fashionable to deride.[10]

Taft was quick to seize the opportunity for a bipartisan alliance with conservative Democrats such as Josiah Bailey and Harry Byrd. Although Bailey's efforts to formalize the Conservative Manifesto in 1937 had proved unsuccessful, Taft was able to build on that earlier effort. The Ohio senator began to display what Kirk and McClellan called "an ability, almost unique among Republicans, to criticize the theories of his opponents while at the same time offering alternatives founded upon much thought and research." The authors explained, "If Taft seemed complex or inconsistent to some critics, it was because, often, they failed to understand that Taft was engaged in applying old principles to new conditions."[11]

Taft's role in solidifying the conservative foundation of the Republican Party and forming a bipartisan conservative coalition in the Senate would have lasting consequences. The coalition of conservative Republicans and Democrats would effectively control the Senate for twenty-five years—long after Taft's death. Gradually, too, conservative southern Democrats would shift into the Republican Party, which Taft revived as the party dedicated to conservative principles. Taft agreed with Tocqueville, who wrote, "The political parties which I call great are those which cling to principles rather than to their consequences, to ideas and not to men."[12] Taft knew that adherence to principle meant sometimes opposing the majority of voters—or even a majority of one's own party members.

"What Is Liberty?"

After less than two years in the Senate, Taft found himself a leading contender for the 1940 Republican presidential nomination. By early 1940 he had toured twenty-eight states and logged more than thirty thousand miles. Press coverage was favorable, and his Ohio-based core group of supporters convinced him to make the run.

The first problem he encountered was his own personality and image. Taft admitted to one news analyst: "I'm afraid you won't find much color in me. I'm too darn normal."[13] There were no funny stories, no catchy sound bites, no slogans; instead he offered a plethora of facts and figures and a careful adherence to basic conservative principles, all delivered in an earnest, flat midwestern drawl. Ever ready with a quip, Alice Roosevelt Longworth, a Taft supporter, could not resist warning the nation that to choose Taft as FDR's replacement would be "like drinking a glass of milk after taking a slug of Benzedrine."[14] One of the best character sketches ever offered of Taft came from the journalist Turner Catledge:

> He was not a warm or genial man—he was cold, and could be extremely hard and righteous—but there was a tremendous honesty about him that commanded respect, and beneath his frigid exterior he was a shy, pleasant sort of man. Sometimes his stubborn honesty

made him seem awkward in the context of the Senate—it was the very opposite of the "to get along, go along" philosophy that prevails in Congress. Bob Taft would not "go along" with anything he was not convinced of after his long and tortuous process of reasoning.[15]

The second hurdle in Taft's path to the presidency in 1940 was substantive. His primary interest and expertise lay in domestic policy, but foreign policy loomed large in 1940. The threat of world war provided FDR with the rationale for a third term and confronted Taft with a tough decision. Though not yet favoring direct intervention in Europe, public opinion was decidedly sympathetic to the Allies. Taft, however, continued to demand a strict hands-off policy. He harbored no sympathy for the dictators, but he firmly believed it was in America's interest to remain neutral. He accused Roosevelt of stirring up public passions and rejected the advice of his staff to do likewise. Catledge saw it clearly: "Taft couldn't shift his views for political expedience, and that was one reason he never captured the Republican nomination."[16]

Taft arrived at the Republican convention in Philadelphia with solid midwestern and southern delegate strength. His rivals were Thomas Dewey, the moderate governor of New York, and Wendell Willkie, a darling of the internationalist, liberal wing of the GOP. A prominent utility company executive, Willkie had never held elective office, but he was a man of considerable charm and charisma—quite unlike Taft or, for that matter, Dewey. On the sixth ballot, with the galleries packed with screaming Willkie supporters, the convention stampeded to nominate "the barefoot boy of Wall Street."

Taft took the defeat philosophically, writing to a relative that as a result of the loss he was likely "to live a longer and happier life." His greatest concern was for his party. With

Willkie, the Republicans had opted to accede to much of the New Deal, and Taft was firmly convinced that this would (and, more important, should) lead to defeat. Taft dutifully supported Willkie's losing campaign against FDR as he returned to the Senate to resume the fight against the New Deal.

His relentless efforts paid off in the 1940s. After the 1942 elections the Republicans still held only thirty-seven Senate seats, but Taft skillfully formed a bipartisan majority with conservative southern Democrats. This coalition blocked every major New Deal domestic initiative during the Second World War, such as the Thomas bill of 1943, which sought federal control of education, and the administration's attempt to use massive subsidies to roll back prices to 1942 levels. In December 1943 journalist Allen Drury wrote in his diary:

> Taft continues to impress me as one of the strongest and ablest members here [the Senate], one of the men who acts consistently as though they think what is being done here really matters to the welfare of the country. Taft, perhaps more than any other, is the leader of the powerful coalition of Republicans and southern Democrats... one of the three or four most powerful men in the United States Senate at the present time.[17]

During the war years, Taft led a vigilant fight to prevent any unnecessary erosion in personal liberty. He was convinced that many in the Roosevelt administration set out to use the war as an excuse to consolidate federal power. In 1942 Taft laid out his concerns: "In our efforts to protect the freedom of this country against aggression from without, we are in a situation today where we must constantly be on guard against suppression of freedom in the United States itself. *We should not go one step in the modification of individual rights beyond what is actually necessary for the war effort*" (emphasis added).[18] Throughout the war he remained fixed on this objective. In late 1943 he wrote:

> What is liberty? It is the freedom of the individual to choose his own work and his life occupation, to spend his earnings as he desires to spend them, to choose the place where he desires to live, to take the job that fits him whether some union official is willing that he get it or not. It is the freedom of cities, of counties, of school districts; the freedom to educate one's children as one thinks best. It is the freedom of thought and experiment in academic institutions. It is the freedom of men in industry to run their business as they think best, so long as they do not interfere with the rights of others to do the same.[19]

As soon as the war ended, Taft demanded that the federal government dismantle wartime controls and regulations. More than any other man, he was responsible for foiling the schemes of the most ardent New Dealers, who sought to accomplish in wartime what they had not been able to accomplish in peacetime.

"Equal Justice under Law"

Undergirding Taft's principles was a reverential respect for the law—the Constitution and the limits it imposed. He stood firmly behind the principle of "equal justice under law"—words engraved on the front of the United States Supreme Court. Whenever the rule of law was at stake, he would speak his mind no matter the political consequences. Such an instance occurred in 1946.

The Western powers were so repulsed by the Nazi atrocities that they determined that the perpetrators would stand trial at Nuremberg for "crimes against humanity." The American public supported the Nuremberg Trials, but Taft knew that the trials violated "that fundamental principle of American law that a man cannot be tried under an ex post facto statute." How, he reasoned, could we fight a war to defend liberty and justice and then impose a settlement on the vanquished that violated those core principles? Political expediency demanded silence, especially with midterm elections less than a month away and control of Congress at stake. But Taft spoke out with force and clarity:

> In these trials we have accepted the Russian idea of the purpose of trials—government policy and not justice—with little relation to Anglo-Saxon heritage. By clothing policy in the forms of legal procedure, we may discredit the whole idea of justice in Europe for years to come.... As I see it, the English-speaking peoples have one great responsibility. That is to restore to the minds of men a devotion to equal justice under law.[20]

Taft's Nuremberg speech outraged many Americans and drew loud denunciations on the campaign trail. Democrats slung charges of anti-Americanism at Taft. Senate Majority Leader Alben Barkley sneered, "Taft never experienced a crescendo of heart about the soup kitchens of 1932, but his heart bled anguishedly for the criminals at Nuremberg." Democrats gloated that Taft's presidential career was over. Meanwhile, Dewey and other Republican leaders disavowed Taft's position. In the face of almost universal criticism, Taft remained calm and resolute. He patiently and rationally reiterated his position, refusing to soften the message in any way.

A decade later, a prominent Democrat would recognize that it took real bravery for Taft to stake out this principled position even though it would threaten his presidential ambitions. John F. Kennedy wrote in *Profiles in Courage*:

> Robert A. Taft was also a man who stuck fast to the basic principles in which he believed—and when those fundamental principles were at issue, not even the lure of the White House, or the possibilities of injuring his candidacy, could deter him from speaking out. He was an able politician, but on more than one occasion he chose to speak out in defense of a position no politician with like ambitions would have endorsed.... Taft had spoken, not in "defense of the Nazi murderers" (as a labor leader charged), not in defense of isolationism (as most observers assumed), but in defense of what he regarded to be the traditional American concepts of law and justice. Justice was at stake, and all other concerns were trivial. As the apostle of strict constitutionalism, Taft was undeterred by the possibilities of injury to his party's precarious position or his own Presidential prospects.[21]

Taft viewed the task of the Republican Party—and his task as congressional leader of the Republican Party—as being to offer the people a reasoned defense of conservative principles and traditional government. In a speech at Yale in 1947 he addressed this challenge: "The American people seem to be doing less and less thinking for themselves and they seem to have less and less knowledge of the history and basic principles of the American Republic. It seems to me that the people have come to form their opinions, not from facts and their own thinking, but from the thinking and opinions of others." As a result, few Americans knew that the Republic was founded "to achieve freedom of thought, freedom of government, and freedom of opportunity." He decried the tendency to judge our society on whether "men have more money, more bathtubs, more automobiles, and less time to work." He continued: "Certainly no one can be against these economic objectives, but it is wrong to subordinate to them the need for greater morality, greater liberty of thought, and greater liberty of action. *I believe that opportunity and not security is still the goal of the American people*" (emphasis added).[22]

Here Taft echoed the message of his conservative predecessors, including Calvin Coolidge and John W. Davis. As we have seen, Coolidge said: "It is only those who do not understand our people, who believe our national life is entirely absorbed by material motives. We make no concealment of the fact that we want wealth, but there are many other things we want much more. We want peace and honor, and that charity which is so strong an element of all civilization."[23] Similarly, Davis had warned: "Whether business is better today than it was yesterday, or will be better or worse tomorrow than it is today, is a poor guide for people who are called upon to decide what sort of government they want to live under. *If they found their government on the shifting sands of unsound principles, it will make no lasting difference whether business is good or bad* [emphasis added]."[24]

Through force of character and intellectual dominance, Taft molded the Republican congressional delegation into a cohesive, conservative force. But he was unable to wrest control of the national party from the eastern, liberal wing. After sitting out the 1944 presidential race and watching FDR defeat Thomas Dewey, Taft mounted vigorous national campaigns in 1948 and again in 1952, only to be deprived of the nomination both times. The pioneering political pollster Samuel Lubell wrote that the GOP's "dilemma has been the necessity of choosing between embracing or repudiating the conservative coalition in Congress."[25]

In each of his three races for the nomination, Taft fell short because the GOP shied away from confronting New Deal liberalism head on and opted for more moderate candidates. Taft, John F. Kennedy wrote, "was never President of the United States. Therein lies his personal tragedy. And therein lies his national greatness."[26] As "Mr. Republican," Taft grounded the GOP in the conservative principles that allowed Barry Goldwater, Ronald Reagan, and other conservative leaders to rise to national power in the coming decades.

"Preserving, Maintaining, and Increasing Liberty"

In 1953, while finally serving as Senate majority leader, Robert Taft was diagnosed with cancer. He died shortly thereafter, at the age of sixty-three. As his father's had, Taft's body lay in state in the U.S. Capitol rotunda while thousands of Americans joined the president, the cabinet, the Supreme Court, and the Congress in paying tribute. Former president Harry Truman, often a political foe, spoke with bipartisan eloquence: "He and I did not agree on public policy, but he knew where I stood and I knew where he stood. We need intellectually honest men like Senator Taft."[27]

Taft, as one of his biographers wrote, "was born to integrity."[28] Over his fourteen years in the Senate, he was known for never breaking his word and never stooping to demagoguery. Several years after his death, a bipartisan senatorial committee announced the selection of the "Five Greatest Senators in U.S. History," and Taft joined John C. Calhoun, Daniel Webster, Henry Clay, and Robert M. La Follette in this august company. Russell Kirk noted, "As much as Calhoun, and more than Webster or Clay, [Taft] declined to sacrifice his principles to prospects of glory."[29] In 1959 a one-hundred-foot tower housing a carillon was erected adjacent to the Capitol to provide a lasting memorial to Taft. But the most fitting memorial can be found in his own simple words inscribed on his tombstone: "The consideration which ought to determine every decision is the necessity of preserving, maintaining, and increasing the liberty of the people of our country."

9

WILLIAM F. BUCKLEY JR., BARRY GOLDWATER, AND RONALD REAGAN

The Conservative Triptych

Although Robert A. Taft managed to forge a conservative coalition in Congress, by the early 1950s the prospects for conservatism did not look promising. New Deal liberalism remained such a dominant political force that intellectuals dismissed conservatism as irrelevant. In 1950 the famous critic Lionel Trilling wrote: "In the United States at this time liberalism is not only the dominant but even the sole intellectual tradition. For it is the plain fact that nowadays there are no conservative or reactionary ideas in general circulation."[1] In 1952 political scientist Herbert McClosky declared that conservatism was to be found "most frequently among the uninformed, the poorly educated, and so far as we can determine, the less intelligent."[2]

The Democratic Party was firmly in the hands of

progressives. Even as Harry Truman's popularity hit new lows, the party embraced his Fair Deal program, the proud successor to the New Deal. John W. Davis, Newton D. Baker, and other conservative Democrats were dying off, and no men of stature took their place on the national stage. The conservative congressional Democratic faction, mostly comprising southerners, could only erect an occasional roadblock to liberal legislation.

Similarly, the Republican Party seemed consigned to a watered-down version of "me-too liberalism." The death of Taft in 1953 and the discrediting of Senator Joseph McCarthy left the GOP in the hands of the eastern liberal establishment. Leaderless, conservatism faced a moribund future.

But suddenly there appeared a young conservative leader of intellect, energy, and vision who breathed new life into a philosophy that was "as old as the Republic itself."

"A Twisted and Ignorant Young Man"

William F. Buckley Jr. was raised in Europe and Connecticut amid privilege and wealth. From his parents he inherited a love of learning, an appreciation of the arts and good living, and a well-defined philosophy of conservatism. William Buckley Sr. was an entrepreneurial Texan who had made and lost a fortune in prerevolutionary Mexico before making another sizable fortune in Europe. His worldview, shaped by his experiences in Mexico, was grounded in individualism, the rule of law, and religiosity.[3]

After a series of tutors and boarding schools, and then service in the U.S. Army, young Bill Buckley enrolled in Yale in 1946. Over his undergraduate career he established himself as a champion debater, the outspoken editor of the *Yale*

Daily News, and an irrepressible evangelist for conservatism in a university dominated by liberal thought. As a debater he developed a signature style that would remain with him for life: his wit was biting, the force of his intellect thoroughly intimidating, and his humor disarming—and devastating.

By his senior year, Buckley was without question the best known and most respected member of his class (for his abilities if not for his ideas). Yale's president asked him to deliver the student address at the annual Alumni Day celebration. Apprehensive about what this known provocateur would say, the administration asked to review Buckley's speech beforehand. The university discovered that Buckley planned to attack with full force what he viewed as Yale's craven abandonment of the tenets of Western civilization and American conservatism. Instead of molding productive leaders for the next American generation, Yale was undermining the very principles upon which the Republic and the university had been founded, Buckley argued in his draft. Fearful of alumni response, the administration demanded substantial revisions. When Buckley refused, Yale withdrew the invitation to speak.

A relieved administration believed it had averted a public relations disaster, but young Buckley was not to be denied. He took his Alumni Day speech notes, expanded them into a two-hundred-page book, including the text of the original Alumni Day speech, and sought out a publisher. Securing the support of a relatively new publisher, Regnery, Buckley raced to get the book out by Yale's 250th anniversary in 1951. Entitled *God and Man at Yale*, the book quickly secured sales from Yale students and alumni, and soon it became apparent that the readership extended far beyond the Yale community. The book surged onto the *New York Times* bestseller list, and within six months more than thirty-five thousand copies had been sold. Both *Time* and *Newsweek* published news stories about Buckley and his book. Yale's efforts to stifle Buckley had instead launched his national career.

It also helped launch a movement. As Austin Bramwell wrote on the fiftieth anniversary of *God and Man at Yale*, Buckley's book stands as "one of the seminal books in modern American conservatism. Without it, one could fairly say, the conservative movement would not exist today."[4] The response of the modern reader to this book is much the same response as to Winston Churchill's first book, *The River War*: incredulity. How could someone in his early twenties have written with such insight and maturity?

In *God and Man at Yale*, Buckley issued a full-throated cry for revolt against the establishment in defending what he defined as Christian individualism: "I believe that the duel between Christianity and atheism is the most important in the world. I further believe that the struggle between individualism and collectivism is the same struggle reproduced on another level."[5] He attacked the Keynesian, collectivist economics that he found pervasively taught at Yale. He lamented that "a Department of Economics that once upheld individual self-reliance and limited government is—but for a few exceptions—now dedicated to collectivism in various degrees."[6] Perhaps most alarming to Yale, Buckley overthrew the conventional notion of academic freedom and insisted that parents and alumni had every right to demand that the university reinforce their basic values. He urged them, as the primary sources of Yale's revenues, to make their voices heard.

The response from Yale and the wider establishment was vitriolic. Yale's new president, Whitney Griswold, assured alumni that he intended "to take the offensive in this matter." Under Griswold's careful supervision, Yale alumnus McGeorge Bundy wrote a scathing three-page review in the *Atlantic*. Bundy not only attacked Buckley's conclusions but also accused him of distortions and shoddy scholarship. He concluded that Buckley was "a twisted and ignorant young man."[7] Yale disseminated some two thousand copies of this review to alumni. Yale trustee Frank Ashburn launched the most virulent attack in *Saturday Review*: "The book is one which has the glow and appeal of a fiery cross on a hillside at night. There will undoubtedly be robed figures who gather to it, but the hoods will not be academic. They will cover the face." Such hysteria dispelled any notion of the reasoned voice of liberalism seeking an open exchange in the marketplace of ideas. The prominent social critic Dwight Macdonald, a Yale alumnus, charged that his alma mater had "reacted with all of the grace and agility of an elephant cornered by a mouse."[8]

Yale had put Buckley in the national spotlight. He soon was named an editor of the *American Mercury*, founded by H. L. Mencken. He became a popular figure on the speaking circuit. He cowrote another book, *McCarthy and His Enemies*. He became president of a new national organization for college students: the Intercollegiate Society of Individualists—later renamed the Intercollegiate Studies Institute. This last act was, as his biographer Lee Edwards points out, "his first conscious act of building a conservative movement."[9]

But by 1955 Buckley had discerned his life's calling: to provide *the* public voice for conservatism.[10] He created a new magazine to advance that cause. From the outset, the goal of *National Review* was both to strengthen conservatism and to influence the course of the nation—and indeed the world.

"What Conservatives Must Decide"

One of Buckley's goals in founding *National Review* was to create a *cohesive* conservative voice. He drew inspiration from different schools of conservative thought: most notably, traditionalism, libertarianism, and anticommunism. With *National Review*, he aimed to convince responsible conservatives of all stripes that they had more in common with one another than with any shade of liberalism. So he courted traditionalists like Russell Kirk, libertarians like John Chamberlain, and anticommunists like Whittaker Chambers to join his new magazine.

Buckley's discussions and correspondence with Chambers, the former Soviet spy turned witness to the dangers of communism, proved especially important to the young editor's view of the magazine. In 1954 Chambers had written to Buckley, "That is what conservatives must decide: how much to give in order to survive at all; how much to give in order not to give up the basic principles."[11] Although he stood always for conservative principles, Buckley also understood the importance of gaining acceptance for conservatism in the political arena. To do so would require weaving together the various strands of conservative thought.

As editor, Buckley presided over *National Review*'s diverse, strong-willed group of editors and writers. He was uniquely equipped to fulfill this role. Although he was not even thirty when the magazine debuted, he was a master diplomat, personally engaging and attractive, a man of impressive intellect who commanded respect from everyone. He consistently hired and retained superb journalistic talent. He was also well connected and able to raise the considerable financial resources required to found and sustain a national publication.

As *National Review* became the leading publication of American conservatism, Buckley himself became the leading spokesman for conservatism. He regularly appeared on TV talk shows, college campuses, and political conferences across the country. He relished the give-and-take of political debate, and his presence on the dais would inevitably draw a crowd.

In September 1960, five years after launching *National Review*, Buckley helped found another significant organization in the conservative movement. He invited more than one hundred conservative student activists from around the country to convene at Great Elm, the Buckley family estate at Sharon, Connecticut. As soon as the talks got under way, Buckley discerned the students' seriousness about seizing the national agenda and effecting conservative reform—"their appetite for power," as he put it. "Ten years ago, the struggle seemed so long, so endless, even we did not dream of victory.... It is quixotic to say that they or their elders have seized the reins of history. But the difference in psychological attitude is tremendous."[12] At these sessions Buckley and the student leaders formed Young Americans for Freedom (YAF) and adopted a charter that came to be known as the Sharon Statement. The charter was pure Buckley: limited government, the centrality of the free market, and the objective of victory in the Cold War.

With the emergence of *National Review*, YAF, and other organizations, conservatism had developed a strong intellectual and political apparatus. Now conservatives needed to find a political leader behind whom the developing conservative movement could rally. Since the death of Taft, no leader had stepped forward. McCarthy was discredited; President Dwight Eisenhower, though personally popular, had done little to strengthen the GOP or to advance conservatism in general; conservatives did not trust Richard Nixon's accommodationist tendencies in both domestic and foreign affairs; and Nelson Rockefeller was hopelessly liberal on domestic issues. Gradually attention began to turn to an attractive, straightforward, consistently conservative westerner, Barry Goldwater.

"The Foremost Conservative Politician in the Nation"

The product of a wealthy Phoenix family, Goldwater was active in business, civic, and political activities in Arizona in the 1930s and 1940s. Goldwater later commented, "I think the foundations of my political philosophy were rooted in my resentment against the New Deal."[13] He involved himself in local and state Republican politics for almost twenty years before running for the U.S. Senate in 1952. Arizona had historically been a Democratic state, but changing demographics and disenchantment with Truman's Fair Deal made the GOP competitive there. Goldwater's announcement for the Senate in 1952 created something of a stir, as the incumbent, Ernest McFarland, was then the Senate majority leader. National GOP leaders, including Illinois senator Everett Dirksen, sensed McFarland's vulnerability and urged Goldwater to run.

With the overwhelming support of the state's leading newspapers, Goldwater hammered McFarland on the issues, which he reduced to the "Three C's: Communism, Cronyism, and Chiseling." Railing against the Democrats' deficit spending, he asked his audience, "You know who's going to pay this bill we've allowed to accumulate, don't you?" And always he supplied the answer: "Our children are going to pay it and live with it for a long time."[14] He waged a well-managed, energetic campaign. A longtime pilot and Air Force veteran, Goldwater flew his private plane into even the remotest regions of Arizona. With the popular Eisenhower as the Republican nominee for president, Goldwater urged Arizonans to "Give Ike a Man He Can Work With."[15] In November, Ike won Arizona by a two-to-one margin, which was just enough to pull in Goldwater by a razor-thin 6,725-vote margin.

In 1953 Goldwater took his Senate seat committed to standing for conservatism. He viewed himself as an outsider: a westerner, a nonlawyer, a businessman, a citizen politician. Unlike Taft, Goldwater was bored by the legislative process; as he had told Arizonans during the Senate campaign and later wrote, "My aim is not to pass laws, but to repeal them."[16] He soon grew disappointed in President Eisenhower's liberal-leaning "me-tooism," and, along with Buckley and other conservatives, he responded with renewed dedication to advancing the conservative agenda. In 1957 Goldwater openly opposed Eisenhower's $71.8 billion budget, blasting the administration as a "dime store version of the New Deal" and accusing the president of "subverting the American economy." Ike was furious, but the *New York Times* recognized that Goldwater and his conservative message had "suddenly arrived" on the national scene in "a spirit of fundamental challenge" to the administration and its "modern Republicanism."[17]

In Eisenhower's second term various elements of the conservative movement began to coalesce. Buckley had a national platform with *National Review,* and he had convinced most conservatives that their fight was against liberals, not among themselves. Conservative radio commentators like former Notre Dame Law School dean Clarence Manion were developing national audiences. Actor Ronald Reagan, host of television's *General Electric Theater,* began traveling the country, speaking at GE plants and hundreds of civic gatherings, to deliver what came to be known among his devotees as "The Speech"—a well-honed, flawlessly delivered compendium of conservative principles. And Goldwater, as chairman of the Republican Senatorial Campaign Committee, traveled to every state delivering his conservative message.

Goldwater biographer Robert Goldberg observed:

Goldwater, Buckley, Reagan, and the other messengers of conservatism labored hard for their beliefs, and their efforts bore fruit. In their hands, conservatism began to lose its hard edge, its coldness, its reputation for being the property of the old, the elite, the rich, and the prejudiced. Conservatives had begun gathering resources and building a movement. Slowly shedding their defensiveness, they felt a heightened self-awareness and confidence, and they basked in a growing visibility.[18]

As the conservative movement took shape, Buckley realized that Goldwater was the most prominent conservative politician to whom the faithful could look for leadership. He and Manion suggested to Goldwater the need for a short statement of his conservative beliefs for campaign purposes. When Goldwater replied that he was not a writer, Buckley filled the void. He assigned his brother-in-law L. Brent Bozell Jr., a *National Review* editor, the task of writing the manifesto, and the result far exceeded their wildest expectations. Written by Bozell with only minor alterations by Goldwater, *The Conscience of a Conservative* was published in 1960. This slim volume almost immediately "made the junior senator from Arizona the foremost conservative politician in the nation," in the words of Buckley biographer Carl Bogus.[19] The book became a national bestseller, went through more than twenty printings, and eventually sold almost four million copies. Years later Pat Buchanan recalled the significance of this book to conservatives: "*The Conscience of a Conservative* was our new testament; it contained the core beliefs of our political faith, it told us why we had failed, what we must do. We read it, memorized it, quoted it.... For those of us wandering in the arid desert of Eisenhower Republicanism, it hit like a rifle shot."[20]

In the introduction, Goldwater set out "to show the connection between Conservative principles, so widely espoused, and Conservative action, so generally neglected." He began with the nature of man as a unique individual created by God in his image. The book described man's economic and spiritual dimensions as "inextricably intertwined," and man as responsible for his own individual development, his own choices, and his own pursuit of happiness. Given this understanding of human nature, the conservative's political objective must be to achieve "the maximum amount of freedom for individuals that is consistent with the maintenance of the social order."

Channeling Jefferson, Goldwater identified government as "the chief instrument for thwarting man's liberty." In a later chapter he declared that "government does not have an unlimited claim on the earnings of individuals" and demanded a clear definition of "the legitimate functions of government." In words that Ronald Reagan would later echo, he concluded:

> And let us by all means remember the nation's interest in reducing taxes and spending. The need for "economic growth" that we hear so much about these days will be achieved, not by the government harnessing the nation's economic forces, but by emancipating them. By reducing taxes and spending we will not only return to the individual the means with which he can assert his freedom and dignity, but also guarantee to the nation the economic strength that will always be its ultimate defense against foreign foes.[21]

"RETURN TO PROVEN WAYS"

Despite the success of *The Conscience of a Conservative*, Goldwater stayed out of the 1960 presidential race. But after

Democrat John F. Kennedy was elected, conservatives sensed an opportunity. New Frontier legislation became bogged down in Congress, blocked by the coalition of Republicans and conservative Democrats. By the fall of 1963, a Draft Goldwater for President Committee, led by political consultant F. Clifton White, was corralling convention delegates. Goldwater's principal opponent for the nomination, liberal New York governor Nelson Rockefeller, was beset by marital problems; other opposition within the GOP was splintered; and opinion polls showed Goldwater within striking distance of Kennedy. Goldwater and Kennedy, who enjoyed a warm personal friendship while maintaining their philosophical differences, even discussed the prospect of running against each other in 1964 and tentatively agreed to a series of Lincoln-Douglas-type debates.[22]

Kennedy traveled to Texas in November 1963 with an eye toward the 1964 campaign. Goldwater was running ahead of Kennedy in Texas polls, and JFK knew he would need to carry the state to secure a convincing mandate for a second term. While on that trip, of course, Kennedy was assassinated. As one of Goldwater's biographers wrote, "The shots in Dallas that snuffed out John Kennedy's life also destroyed any chance Barry Goldwater had of being president of the United States."[23]

In the aftermath of the assassination, Goldwater seriously considered dropping out of the race. He noted that he and Kennedy had been "personal friends" and said, "It is a great loss to the nation and to me."[24] He had relished the idea of opposing Kennedy, a man he enjoyed and respected, while he held Lyndon Johnson in low esteem. He knew Johnson to be a devious politician and an unprincipled opportunist. He also believed the nation would accord Johnson a "honeymoon" period that would extend beyond the upcoming election. Only reluctantly did Goldwater accede to the pleas of his partisans to run.

As the fight for the GOP nomination unfolded, two factors defined the story. First, Goldwater's penchant for candor became a liability. Kennedy had predicted this, saying: "If he's the nominee, people will start asking him questions, and he's so damned quick on the trigger that he will answer them. And when he does, it will be over."[25] In a series of exchanges with the press, Goldwater gave unrehearsed answers that led to widespread misrepresentation and misinterpretation. The press liked Goldwater personally but was merciless in characterizing him as "trigger happy." This image was soon etched in the public consciousness.

Second, Nelson Rockefeller and another liberal candidate, Pennsylvania governor William Scranton, launched vicious attacks on Goldwater in a desperate attempt to secure the GOP nomination. Their campaigns characterized Goldwater as dangerously radical, intellectually shallow, and psychologically unstable. Despite their increasingly frantic efforts, Goldwater had the nomination sewed up after his narrow victory over Rockefeller in the California primary in June. The eastern GOP liberals could not believe the party would turn its back on the Eisenhower legacy and reject their decades-long control of the national party. Instead of calling for party unity, they continued to hammer Goldwater up to and during the Republican convention that July, painting him as an extremist who sought to hijack the party. Before the general election began, Goldwater's fellow Republicans had already done the Democrats' work in tarnishing his image.

The "stop Goldwater" movement reached its apogee with the infamous "Scranton letter." Goldwater had known Bill Scranton for years, serving with him in the same Air Force reserve unit, and he held Scranton in high regard. He had even urged the Pennsylvanian to run for president in 1963 and was considering him as a vice-presidential running mate.

But on July 12, the day before the convention opened, Goldwater received a scathing letter from the Scranton campaign and bearing Scranton's signature. The letter accused Goldwater of espousing "radical extremism," nuclear "irresponsibility," and racial bigotry.[26] Realizing the letter was ill conceived, Scranton tried to distance himself from it, saying his aides had sent it without securing his approval. But the damage was done. Goldwater was furious at the injustice of the charges, and his followers were seething with indignation.

The convention became a public relations disaster for Goldwater and the Republicans—but also a watershed in the history of the GOP and the nation. Goldwater's delegates were in no mood to compromise on the party platform, and the gallery booed Rockefeller when he pushed for a more liberal plank. President Eisenhower delivered a speech intended to foster party unity. It was an undistinguished speech that did little to excite the delegates—until Eisenhower digressed with the following comment: "So let us particularly scorn the divisive efforts of those outside our family, including sensation-seeking columnists and commentators... men and women who couldn't care less about the good of our party."[27] This attack on the press energized Goldwater's conservatives, prompting an eruption from the floor that lasted fifteen minutes. The outburst left a befuddled Ike standing at the podium while the party chairman frantically banged the gavel in a futile effort to restore order. Henry Cabot Lodge, the stuffy Boston Brahmin and quintessential liberal Republican, was heard to mutter as he hurried out of San Francisco's Cow Palace, "What in God's name has happened to the Republican Party! I hardly know any of these people!"[28] Lodge's comment was prescient: the Republican Party had moved to the right, and the ruling eastern establishment had been unwilling to acknowledge or accommodate the shift.

As Goldwater prepared his acceptance speech to the convention, he saw no reason to dilute his conservative message. He had long thought that President Lyndon Johnson would defeat any Republican nominee in 1964, less than a year after JFK's assassination. And now that his fellow Republicans had destroyed his credibility, he saw the purpose of his campaign as to delineate a conservative agenda for the future. From the moment he stepped to the podium, it was clear that Goldwater was issuing a call to arms. He began: "Our people have followed false prophets. We must and we shall return to proven ways—not because they are old, but because they are true." Throughout the speech he used words like *freedom*, *liberty*, *honesty*, *constitutional*, and *destiny*. Goldwater's acceptance speech was, in Buckley's words, "an expression of contempt for and defiance of the critics" that culminated in "the most notorious rhetorical couplet in modern political history."[29] Buckley's characterization of this couplet was not exaggerated: "I would remind you that extremism in the defense of liberty is no vice. And let me remind you also that moderation in the pursuit of justice is no virtue."

The delegates in San Francisco responded deliriously: Goldwater was not giving an inch. But the press had the opposite reaction. Political journalist Theodore White, who was covering the convention for one of the major networks, gasped, "My God, he's really going to run as Barry Goldwater!"[30] Despite *National Review*'s valiant effort to show that Goldwater's words were similar to those of Thomas Paine, William Gladstone, Wendell Willkie, and even Martin Luther King Jr., that couplet in the acceptance speech branded Goldwater as a dangerous extremist.

In the ensuing weeks, Goldwater tried to focus his campaign on the most conservative issues: reducing the size of government, lowering taxes, strengthening the military, and adhering to strict constructionism. He flouted conventional electoral wisdom: He went into Tennessee and called for the privatization of the New Deal's Tennessee Valley Authority. In Florida, before thousands of retirees, he advocated Social Security reform. In Michigan, home to the powerful United Auto Workers, he praised right-to work legislation. In Appalachia he denounced the War on Poverty. As Lee Edwards wrote, "the battle was joined between a candidate for whom winning the presidency was not everything and a candidate for whom winning the presidency was the only thing."[31] Lyndon Johnson, knowing his advantage, refused Goldwater's challenge to debate the issues. The president distilled his message down to these simple words that emphasized his own leadership and cast doubt on Goldwater's: "Now you take care of me and I'll take care of you for the next four years.... Vote to save your Social Security from going down the drain. Vote to keep a prudent hand which will not mash the nuclear button."

Enter Reagan, Stage Right

In October, as Goldwater faced almost-certain defeat, a group of wealthy California businessmen decided to make a last-ditch effort on his behalf and, perhaps more important, to end the campaign with an articulate appeal for the future. These businessmen bought national TV time and proposed to Goldwater's campaign that Ronald Reagan make the appeal, which was entitled "A Time for Choosing." Goldwater's campaign managers initially rejected the offer, but when the candidate reviewed the taped message, he immediately saw its potential and approved it. Goldwater demanded of his feckless managers, "What the hell's wrong with that?"

Broadcast on October 27, one week before the election,

Reagan's speech was the stump version of Goldwater's book. In plain language he laid out the conservative message:

> You and I are told increasingly we have to choose between a left or right. Well, I'd like to suggest there is no such thing as a left or right. There's only an up or down—up to man's age-old dream, the ultimate in individual freedom consistent with law and order—or down to the ant heap of totalitarianism. And regardless of their sincerity, their humanitarian motives, those who would trade our freedom for security have embarked on this downward course.

After thoughtfully outlining the argument for reducing the size, scope, and intrusiveness of government, Reagan concluded with these words: "You and I have a rendezvous with destiny. We'll preserve for our children this, the last best hope of man on earth, or we'll sentence them to take the last step into a thousand years of darkness."[32]

The response was dramatic. Polls reported an astounding 15 percent shift from Johnson to Goldwater among respondents who viewed the speech. More than $500,000 in individual contributions poured into the Republican campaign. This speech was the high point of Goldwater's campaign—and it launched Reagan's political career. Political reporter David Broder pronounced it "the most successful national political debut since William Jennings Bryan electrified the 1896 Democratic convention."[33]

Election Day 1964 produced a landslide of mammoth proportions: Johnson carried all but six states and won the popular vote by 61.1 to 38.5 percent. Pundits predicted (not for the last time) the death of conservatism. James Reston of the *New York Times* wrote: "Barry Goldwater not only lost the Presidential election yesterday but the conservative cause as well. He has wrecked his party for a long time to come and is not even likely to control the wreckage."[34] Reston's *Times* colleague Tom Wicker had similar thoughts: "The Republicans cannot win in this era of American history except as a me-too party." The dean of American commentators, Walter Lippmann, wrote, "The Johnson majority is indisputable proof that the voters are in the center."[35] The *Saturday Evening Post* predicted that the Goldwater defeat would "drive the fanatic saboteurs of the Republican Party back into the woodwork whence they came."[36] Several years later the liberal historian Arthur Schlesinger Jr. delivered this postmortem: "The election results of 1964 seemed to demonstrate Thomas Dewey's prediction about what would happen if the parties were realigned on an ideological basis: 'The Democrats would win every election and the Republicans would lose every election.'"[37] Scarcely a voice was heard to raise a contrarian assessment.

Two Campaigns

It fell to Buckley and Reagan to bind up the wounds of the faithful and call them to renewed action. Buckley began his mission even before the November defeat. On September 11, 1964, at the YAF national convention in New York, Buckley spoke soberly of the upcoming election: "A great rainfall has deluged a thirsty earth, but before we had time properly to prepare the ground. I speak of course about the impending defeat of Barry Goldwater." This statement was met with a hushed silence. But Buckley inspired the young partisans by calling for "cultivating in the Goldwater camp the morale of an army on the march." He reminded them, "The glorious development of this year was the nomination of a man whose views have given the waiting community a choice." He concluded by saying that although the walls of liberalism would stand "firm against our assault" in 1964, after Election Day "we must emerge smiling, confident in the knowledge that we weakened those walls, that they will never again stand so firmly against us."[38] After the election, Buckley wrote movingly of Goldwater as a man "who had defied American taboos by running for president without compromising his principles." He added, "No one else comes to mind who sustained for so long a comparable reputation for candor and courage."[39] On the morning after the election, Reagan offered consolation to his fellow conservatives: "We're just starting out. God bless all of you and I'm sure that in the days ahead we won't lack for ammunition."[40]

By January 1965, Clif White had convened a group of former Draft Goldwater leaders for the purpose of convincing Reagan to run for office. These conservatives, along with a group of wealthy California industrialists, persuaded the reluctant actor to run for governor of California in 1966. Simultaneously, Buckley was considering a run for mayor of New York City on the Conservative Party ticket. He reasoned that conservatism needed a new face following the Goldwater defeat, and where better to join the fight than in the heart of eastern liberalism.

As *National Review*'s John O'Sullivan later wrote, Buckley mounted a serious campaign "disguised as a lark."[41] When a reporter asked the first thing he would do if elected mayor, Buckley replied with his most memorable quote: "Demand a recount."[42] Proving that conservatism could be fun was accomplishment enough, but Buckley also used the mayoral campaign to advance serious conservative proposals. He introduced the revolutionary concepts of "workfare" and enterprise zones, for example. With his thoughtful proposals, command of the facts, and irreverent wit, Buckley drew attention away from, and cast doubts on, the Republican candidate—the handsome congressman John Lindsay, darling of the GOP left wing. (Lindsay also ran on the Liberal Party's ticket.) On Election Day, Buckley garnered more than 13 percent of the vote—impressive for a third-party effort—while Lindsay barely defeated the lackluster Democratic candidate, Abe Beame, 45 percent to 41 percent.

Meanwhile in California, Reagan was proving to be a consummate campaigner. He was able to take Goldwater's principles and present them in such a reassuring way that his liberal opponents seemed misguided when they tried to label him "a Goldwater extremist." Reagan demonstrated a serious grasp of the issues and a firm grounding in conservative principles, which was the result of years of study and speaking on the public circuit for General Electric. His Democratic opponent, incumbent governor Edmund "Pat" Brown, who had defeated Richard Nixon in 1962, seriously underestimated Reagan's intellectual depth and political ability. The liberal Brown could not believe that "a Goldwater radical" could ever be elected governor of the progressive state of California—and certainly not a worn-out old B-movie actor. The governor explained that he had been addressing the state's political and social problems while Reagan had been filming *Bedtime for Bonzo*.

In November, an astounded Governor Brown found himself one million votes behind in a Reagan landslide.

"An Inspirational Voice to America"

As the governor of the nation's most populous state, Reagan immediately became a force in national politics and a leading conservative spokesman. His strong leadership in addressing California's major economic problems positioned Reagan as a potential presidential candidate in 1968. Despite having served little more than a year as governor, he emerged as the main rival to Richard Nixon in the primaries. Nixon won the nomination and was elected president that fall. Reagan rejected an offer to join the new administration and opted to run for gubernatorial reelection in 1970. He won that race, too, and after serving eight years as governor, he chose not to run for reelection again. Reagan rejected another presidential overture to come to Washington—this time from President Gerald Ford. Instead he committed to an ambitious national speaking tour, a column, and radio commentaries that cemented his standing as the country's leading conservative politician.

Reagan sensed Ford's vulnerability and waged a vigorous campaign to unseat the incumbent in 1976. As early as the summer of 1975, Buckley was writing about Reagan's strong potential as a candidate: "Reagan's threat to Ford is that he was born with an uncanny ability to persuade: to marshal his arguments in a way that combines drama and didacticism. I have, in my extensive experience listening to public speakers, come across only one or two people who are his match."[43] The threat proved real: Reagan came within a mere handful of delegates of taking the Republican nomination from Ford. His concession speech at the convention left many delegates and commentators convinced that Reagan would have been a far stronger candidate than the likeable but feckless Jerry Ford. Democrat Jimmy Carter defeated Ford that fall.

As the 1980 election approached, Reagan knew that, because of his age, this would be his last chance at the presidency. He was fortunate in both his opponent and his timing. Under Carter, the public sensed that domestic economic and foreign policy conditions were spiraling out of control. The "misery index," which showed the dual ravages of inflation and unemployment, reached record highs, and the president could only bemoan a sense of "national malaise." Meanwhile, the Soviets had invaded Afghanistan and Iranian extremists had stormed the U.S. Embassy in Tehran, taking fifty-two Americans hostage; the rescue mission Carter authorized failed miserably.

In these demoralizing conditions, a confident, articulate Reagan stepped forward. He easily secured the GOP nomination and, unlike Goldwater, ran an impressive general election campaign. He not only delivered eloquent prepared addresses but also—much to the Democrats' surprise—proved effective in a series of debates with Carter. He presented himself, the challenger, as genuinely presidential while diminishing the stature of the president, who seemed petty and defensive. Once again, his opponents vastly underestimated Reagan's ability to deflect criticisms—concerns about his age, reactionary policies, intellectual shallowness—and to connect with the public in lucid explanations of conservative principles. Election Day brought a landslide: Reagan won the popular vote by a ten-point margin and the electoral vote 489–49. Years later, Jimmy Carter summed up the race: "President Reagan was a formidable campaigner who provided an inspirational voice to America when our people were searching for a clear message of hope and confidence."[44]

"GOVERNMENT IS NOT THE SOLUTION TO OUR PROBLEM"

The public did not have to wait long to know what Reagan intended to deliver. His inaugural address, January 20, 1981, was unambiguous: "In this present crisis, government is not the solution to our problem; government is the problem." In words reminiscent of those of Grover Cleveland and Calvin

Coolidge, he extolled limited government: "It is my intention to curb the size and the influence of the federal establishment and to demand recognition of the distinction between the powers granted to the federal government and those reserved to the states or to the people." In conclusion, he offered inspiring words that would underlie both his domestic and foreign policies: "We must realize that no arsenal, or no weapon in the arsenals of the world, is so formidable as the will and moral courage of free men and women."[45]

Within minutes of concluding the speech, Reagan directed the White House curator to hang the portrait of Coolidge in the Cabinet Room. Several weeks later, Reagan explained the decision to a perplexed *Newsweek* reporter: "If you go back, I don't know if the country has ever had a higher level of prosperity than it did under Coolidge. And he actually reduced the national debt, he cut taxes several times across the board. And maybe the criticism was in both cases that they weren't activist enough. Well, maybe there's a lesson in that. Maybe we've had instances of government being too active, intervening, interfering."[46] It was clear from the beginning: this president was on a conservative course.

Every administration has its defining moments. The first for Reagan's arrived in August 1981. In violation of the law prohibiting strikes by public employee unions, the Professional Air Traffic Controllers Organization (PATCO) called a strike on August 3, seeking higher pay and reduced hours. PATCO had been one of the few unions to support Reagan's candidacy in 1980; its leadership may have expected to extract some benefit in return for that political support. But Reagan, acting under the Taft-Hartley Act of 1947, ordered the strikers back to work, declaring the strike "a peril to national safety." When only 10 percent of the strikers complied, Reagan gave the strikers forty-eight hours in which to return or face forfeiture of their jobs. Simultaneously, the government began to implement a contingency plan to restore partial flight operations. On August 5 the workers refused to return to work. Reagan fired all 11,345 strikers.

At the end of August, a *New York Times* editorial warned of public "uneasiness over the harshness of his [Reagan's] actions" and recommended that the president "allow strikers to go back to work—but with some penalties."[47] Despite this public pressure, Reagan stayed the course. In assuring his transportation secretary of his continuing support, Reagan quoted Coolidge from the Boston Police Strike: "There is no right to strike against the public safety by anybody, anywhere, at any time."[48]

The PATCO episode sent a powerful message that this administration meant what it said and would not back away from its principled positions—a message delivered to political allies and opponents not only at home but abroad as well. Reagan's last secretary of state, George Shultz, termed the PATCO action the "most important foreign policy decision Ronald Reagan ever made."[49]

Reagan also clearly established his economic policy during his first year in office. In 1980 he had campaigned on a four-point economic policy platform: reduction in the growth of government, reduction in tax rates on income and capital gains, reduction in inflation by tightening the money supply, and reduction in regulation of business. Despite the positive economic results following the Coolidge tax cuts in the mid-1920s and the Kennedy tax cuts in the early 1960s, conventional Republicans remained skeptical of tax cuts, fearing inflationary effects. Reagan's own vice president, George H. W. Bush, had blasted Reagan's supply-side policies as "voodoo economics" during the 1980 Republican primaries. In 1981 Reagan mobilized public opinion in favor of across-the-board tax cuts, convinced the GOP to support him, and cajoled a reluctant Congress into action. Top marginal tax rates on individual income ultimately fell from more than 70 percent to 24 percent under Reagan. Similarly, Reagan's administration reduced the annual growth rate in federal spending from an average of 4 percent under Carter to 2.5 percent. In fighting inflation, Reagan gave strong support to Federal Reserve chairman Paul Volcker's tight-money policies, which succeeded in taming inflation. Support for this tight-money policy, which manifested itself in record-high interest rates, cost Reagan and the GOP public support in the 1982 off-year elections, but Reagan never flinched. Finally, the Reagan administration made a concentrated effort to reduce bloated regulations, retract the reach of government oversight, and establish business confidence. The result of this four-pronged policy was the second-longest peacetime economic expansion in American history.

Reagan's years were also marked by tremendous success in foreign policy. Through a combination of increased defense spending and strategically significant actions in relatively minor clashes (for example, the Granada invasion and the bombing of Libya), Reagan convinced the Soviets that he was not posturing when he said his Cold War strategy was simply "to win." As with domestic policy, Reagan's foreign policy began with some core convictions. He genuinely believed in the "American dream." In fact, as his speechwriter Peggy Noonan has written, Reagan believed that he "was living proof of the American dream."[50] Because he believed so fervently in individual freedom, he viewed communism as evil. He could look at the Berlin Wall with only one thought: "This wall will fall. For it cannot withstand faith; it cannot withstand truth. The wall cannot withstand freedom."[51]

As Reagan prepared to step down as president in January 1989, he and his fellow conservatives could look back over

eight years of enormous accomplishment. Both his economic and foreign policies had achieved remarkable results. On the domestic front, he had confronted the conventional wisdom that the growth of government was inevitable. Although he was frustrated at his inability to reduce government spending more radically, Reagan did slow the growth of government and restore confidence and optimism to the private sector. In foreign affairs, Reagan could justifiably muse, "We meant to change a nation, and instead we changed a world." With the critical support of British prime minister Margaret Thatcher and Pope John Paul II, Reagan won the Cold War: less than a year after he left office, the Berlin Wall fell.

Reagan's defining combination of virtues made all of these momentous achievements possible. He brought to the presidency an unyielding commitment to core conservative principles, an exceptional ability to communicate these principles in language the American public could understand and embrace, and an unfailing personal civility and graciousness. Those last virtues should not be underestimated. Buckley once observed that Reagan was "almost certainly the nicest man who ever occupied the White House."[52] A close personal friend of Reagan offered this observation: "The key about Ronnie is this: I knew him as a movie actor, as a governor of the state of California, as president of the United States, and the thing about him is he never changed. He was humble. He had no sense of entitlement. It wasn't about him, ever."[53]

Buckley summed up the president's impact: "Reagan's period was brief, but he did indeed put his stamp on it. He did this in part because he was scornful of the claims of omnipotent government, in part because he felt, and expressed, the buoyancy of the American Republic."[54]

Ronald Reagan changed the country and, indeed, the world. But his legacy to conservatism deserves notice as well. While being the object of the intellectual establishment's scorn, he managed to make conservative philosophy, which had supposedly been buried in the Johnson landslide of 1964, part of the American mainstream.

"Committed to Great Ideas"

Together, Buckley, Goldwater, and Reagan form the modern conservative triptych. Their lives were intricately interwoven over the last half of the twentieth century. Buckley profoundly influenced the thought of Goldwater and Reagan, and he served as an informal adviser to both. John O'Sullivan pointed out: "Reagan's victory was the triumph of Bill Buckley's philosophy and a catastrophic defeat for the suffocating liberalism that had dominated America in 1951. The rest was details."⁵⁵ Meanwhile, the public careers of Goldwater and Reagan contributed incalculably to Buckley's impact and reach. As *The Economist* wrote in 2014, "The ideas Barry Goldwater set forth in *The Conscience of a Conservative* led to him losing 44 of the 50 states in the 1964 presidential election. But it is striking how much of what the candidate wanted the country eventually got."⁵⁶ And the conservative philosophy that Buckley and Goldwater stood for never would have assumed such influence were it not for a political leader with the vision, talent, character, and resolve of Reagan. Buckley wrote admiringly: "Ronald Reagan had strategic visions. He told us that most of our civic problems were problems brought on or exacerbated by government, not problems that could be solved by government." For Buckley, Reagan "incarnated American ideals at many levels."⁵⁷

Reagan might well have spoken for all three of these giants of twentieth-century conservatism when he said of himself: "I never thought of myself as a great man, just a man committed to great ideas. I've always believed that individuals should take priority over the state. History has taught me that this is what sets America apart—not to remake the world in our image, but to inspire people everywhere with a sense of their own boundless possibilities."⁵⁸

Epilogue
"AS OLD AS THE REPUBLIC ITSELF"

In profiling this "faithful band" of conservatives, I hope I have enabled readers to absorb and apply the principles of conservatism just a bit better. Different as these fourteen American leaders may have been, they were united in their commitment to a political philosophy "as old as the Republic itself." Each made his mark on conservatism and on the country.

Having considered the lives and careers of these fourteen American statesmen, I leave you with the following three thoughts:

First, ideas have consequences. One's beliefs about central issues shape his worldview and dictate his course of action. The conservative philosophy that is traced in this book has survived because it is based on fundamental truths, and throughout American history leaders such as those profiled here have applied timeless conservative principles to the challenges and crises of their age.

Second, it is important to study history. "Study history, study history," Winston Churchill advised. "In history lie all the secrets of statecraft." History is the story of the ideas, actions, triumphs, and defeats of individuals. As Harry Truman once noted, "Men make history and not the other way around." To know where we should go, it is essential to know where we have been.

Finally, although the modern examples may be few, graciousness and civility are not outdated political attributes. Strong conviction does not preclude these attributes; likewise, civility and graciousness do not demand philosophical ambivalence. Despite all the unattractiveness of modern politics, Lord Tweedsmuir's famous statement still holds: "Public life is regarded as the crown of a career, and to young men [and women] it is the worthiest ambition. Politics is still the greatest and most honorable adventure."

Notes

INTRODUCTION: "A FAITHFUL BAND"

1 Newton D. Baker, "Introduction," *The Cabinet Diary of William L. Wilson* (Chapel Hill: University of North Carolina Press, 1957), xxv.
2 Amity Shlaes, *The Forgotten Man* (New York: HarperCollins, 2007), 11.
3 Political labels are fluid and thus can never be exact. Many of the figures profiled in this book did not embrace the name "conservative." Calvin Coolidge and Grover Cleveland often described their philosophies simply as "common sense." John W. Davis, a leading lawyer and politician who was raised as a Jeffersonian liberal, wrote to a friend in 1937: "I have never thought of myself as an indurated Tory. On the contrary, I have gloried in the name of liberal, which I interpret to mean a love for the greatest liberty consistent with public order. The great trouble with our modern 'liberals' is that they think liberalism means exceeding liberality with other people's money." The great twentieth-century economist and philosopher F. A. Hayek refused to be called a conservative, insisting

on being known as an "Old Whig." Robert A. Taft referred to himself as a "conservative liberal." Today, some label themselves "libertarians"; others, "traditionalists."

4 Andrew Schlesinger and Stephen Schlesinger, eds., *The Letters of Arthur Schlesinger Jr.* (New York: Random House, 2013), 245.
5 Arthur Schlesinger Jr., *Cycles of American History* (New York: Mariner Books, 1999), 62.
6 Thomas B. Silver, *Coolidge and the Historians* (Durham, NC: Carolina Academic Press, 1982), 137.
7 Allan Nevins and Henry Steele Commager, *A Pocket History of the United States* (New York: Washington Square Press, 1967), 410, 420.
8 Arthur Schlesinger Jr., *The Coming of the New Deal, 1933–1935* (New York: Mariner Books, 2003), 588.
9 Paul Johnson, *A History of the American People* (New York: HarperCollins, 1997), 718.
10 Shlaes, *The Forgotten Man*, 9. See also Jim Powell, *FDR's Folly* (New York: Crown Forum, 2003), and Burton W. Folsom, *New Deal or Raw Deal?* (New York: Threshold, 2008).
11 Myron Magnet, *The Founders at Home* (New York: W. W. Norton, 2013), 9.
12 Alexander Hamilton, James Madison, John Jay, *The Federalist Papers*, No. 6.
13 *Modern Age* 29, no. 4 (Fall 1985): 295.
14 Russell Kirk, *The Roots of American Order* (Wilmington, DE: ISI Books, 2003), 29.
15 Russell Kirk and James McClellan, *The Political Principles of Robert A. Taft* (New York: Fleet Press, 1967), 3. The words quoted here are Kirk and McClellan's summary of Taft's view.
16 Thomas Jefferson, First Inaugural Address, March 4, 1801, available from the Avalon Project at Yale University, avalon.law.yale.edu/19th_century/jefinau1.asp.
17 Johnson, *A History of the American People*, 212.
18 Stuart Bruchey, *Enterprise: The Dynamic Economy of a Free People* (Cambridge, MA: Harvard University Press, 1990), 559.
19 *New York Times*, March 5, 1933.
20 *Federalist* No. 6.
21 Alexis de Tocqueville, *Democracy in America* (New York: Barnes and Noble Books, 2003), 178, 38.
22 *Wall Street Journal*, March 26, 1997.
23 Russell Kirk, *The Conservative Mind* (Washington, DC: Regnery Publishing, 1985), 28.

24 Edmund Burke, *Reflections on the Revolution in France* (Oxford: Oxford University Press, 1993), 246.
25 Kirk, *The Conservative Mind*, 32.
26 Winston S. Churchill, House of Commons, March 14, 1938.

CHAPTER 1: THOMAS JEFFERSON AND JAMES MADISON

1 Letter, James Madison to Thomas Jefferson, April 23, 1787, in *The Republic of Letters*, ed. James Morton Smith (New York: W. W. Norton, 1995), 1:439.
2 Letter, James Madison to George Washington, March 18, 1787, in *The Papers of James Madison Digital Edition*, ed. J.C.A. Stagg (Charlottesville: University of Virginia Press, 2010), rotunda. upress.virginia.edu/founders/JSMN.
3 Letter, James Madison to John G. Jackson, December 27, 1821, in *The Writings of James Madison*, ed. Gaillard Hunt (New York: G. P. Putnam's Sons, 1910), 9:72.
4 Letter, James Madison to George Washington, February 21, 1787, in *The Papers of James Madison Digital Edition*.
5 See *Federalist* No. 40.
6 Letter, James Madison to George Washington, April 16, 1787, in *The Papers of James Madison Digital Edition*.
7 Letter, Thomas Jefferson to James Madison, June 20, 1787, in *The Republic of Letters*, 1:443.
8 William Pierce, "Character Sketches of Delegates of the Federal Convention," in *The Republic of Letters*, 1:444.
9 Letter, Thomas Jefferson to James Madison, October 24, 1787, in *The Republic of Letters*, 1:446.
10 Letter, Thomas Jefferson to John Adams, November 13, 1787, in Mary A. Giunta, ed., *Documents of the Emerging Nation* (Wilmington, DE: Scholarly Resources, 1998), 262.
11 Letter, Thomas Jefferson to James Madison, December 20, 1787, in *The Republic of Letters*, 1:450.
12 Ibid.
13 Letter, Thomas Jefferson to Abigail Adams, February 22, 1787, in *The Republic of Letters*, 1:439.
14 *Federalist* No. 10, No. 14.
15 *Federalist* No. 45.
16 Letter, James Madison to Thomas Jefferson, February 4, 1790, in *The Republic of Letters*, 1:650.

17 James Madison, Speech in Congress Opposing the National Bank, February 2, 1791, in *The Papers of James Madison*, ed. William T. Hutchinson et al. (Chicago: University of Chicago Press, 1962–77), 3:244–45.
18 Thomas Jefferson, "Opinion on the Constitutionality of a National Bank," February 15, 1791, available from the Avalon Project at Yale University, avalon.law.yale.edu/18th_century/bank-tj.asp.
19 *National Gazette*, January 19, 1792, in *The Writings of James Madison*, 6:85.
20 *Annals of Congress of the United States*, III:363ff.
21 "Alien and Sedition Acts of 1798," Nolo.com, www.nolo.com/legal-encyclopedia/content/alien-sedition-act.html.
22 Thomas Jefferson, "Kentucky Resolutions," in *The Republic of Letters*, 1080.
23 Ibid.
24 James Madison, "Virginia Resolutions," in *The Republic of Letters*, 1101.
25 Ryan S. Walters, *The Last Jeffersonian* (Bloomington, IN: Westbow Press, 2012), 19, 71. On whether Jefferson ever made that precise statement, see, e.g., the Thomas Jefferson Foundation's research into the quotation. The statement has not been located in Jefferson's writings, but in 1837 a Jacksonian editor wrote a close variation: "The best government is that which governs least" (*United States Magazine and Democratic Review* 1, no. 1 [1837]: 6). The Jefferson Foundation's research can be found at www.monticello.org/site/jefferson/government-best-which-governs-least-quotation.
26 Jefferson, First Inaugural Address.

Chapter 2: Nathaniel Macon and John Randolph

1 *Annals of Congress of the United States*, 5th Congress, 3rd session, 2493.
2 William E. Dodd, *The Life of Nathaniel Macon* (Raleigh, NC: Edwards & Broughton, 1903), 138.
3 John Wheeler, *Historical Sketches of North Carolina* (Philadelphia: Lippincott, Grambo, 1851), 433.
4 Dodd, *The Life of Nathaniel Macon*, 154.
5 Ibid., 145.
6 F. W. Thomas, *John Randolph, of Roanoke, and Other Sketches of Character* (Philadelphia: A. Hart, 1853), 14–16.

7 *Annals of Congress of the United States*, 6th Congress, 1st session, 298.
8 Ibid., 149.
9 Dodd, *The Life of Nathaniel Macon*, 174.
10 *Annals of Congress of the United States*, 7th Congress, 1st session, 366.
11 *Annals of Congress of the United States*, 8th Congress, 1st session, 998.
12 St. George Tucker, *A Dissertation on Slavery* (Philadelphia: Matthew Carey, 1796), 3.
13 Register of Debates, 19th Congress, 1st session, 118.
14 Russell Kirk, *John Randolph of Roanoke* (Indianapolis: Liberty Fund, 1997), 179.
15 Ibid.
16 Dodd, *The Life of Nathaniel Macon*,198.
17 *Annals of Congress of the United States*, 17th Congress, 1st session, 943.
18 Henry Adams, *John Randolph* (Boston: Houghton Mifflin, 1892), 53.
19 Thomas P. Abernethy, *The South in the New Nation, 1789–1819* (Baton Rouge: Louisiana State University Press, 1961), 314.
20 Kirk, *John Randolph of Roanoke*, 153
21 Edward R. Cotten, *Life of Nathaniel Macon* (Philadelphia: Lippincott, 1840), 55.
22 *Proceedings of the Virginia State Convention*, 801.
23 Kirk, *The Conservative Mind*, 158.
24 Letter, Nathaniel Macon to Martin Van Buren, May 24, 1836, North Carolina State Department of Archives.
25 Letter, Nathaniel Macon to N. Weldon Edwards, March 3, 1828, North Carolina State Department of Archives.
26 Dodd, *The Life of Nathaniel Macon*, 182.
27 William Cabell Bruce, *John Randolph of Roanoke, 1773–1833* (New York: G. P. Putnam's Sons, 1922), 1:427.
28 Letter, Nathaniel Macon to Weldon Edwards, February 17, 1828, North Carolina State Department of Archives.
29 Cotten, *Life of Nathaniel Macon*, 151.
30 Kirk, *John Randolph of Roanoke*, 153.
31 Adams, *John Randolph*, 39.
32 Kirk, *John Randolph of Roanoke*, 220.
33 Nathan Loughborough, "Notes on Randolph," Manuscript, Library of Virginia.
34 Wheeler, *Historical Sketches of North Carolina*, 434.
35 Letter, Thomas Jefferson to Nathaniel Macon, March 24, 1826, quoted in Thomas Hart Benton, "Nathaniel Macon," in W. J. Peele, ed., *Lives of Distinguished North Carolinians* (Raleigh: North Carolina Publishing Society, 1898), 95.

Chapter 3: John C. Calhoun

1. Christopher Hollis, *The American Heresy* (New York: Minton, Balch, 1939), 98.
2. Ibid.
3. *The Papers of John C. Calhoun*, ed. Clyde N. Wilson and W. Edwin Hemphill (Columbia: University of South Carolina Press), 10:307.
4. *Niles Weekly Register*, August 4, 1827.
5. Margaret Coit, *John C. Calhoun* (Boston: Houghton Mifflin, 1950), 170.
6. Ibid.
7. Irving H. Bartlett, *John C. Calhoun: A Biography* (New York: W. W. Norton, 1993), 147.
8. "Exposition and Protest," *John C. Calhoun: Selected Writings and Speeches*, ed. H. Lee Cheek Jr. (Washington, DC: Regnery Publishing, 2003), 271.
9. Ibid., 275.
10. Ibid., 274.
11. Ibid., 288.
12. Ibid., 289.
13. Ibid., 292.
14. Ibid., 295, 297.
15. Ibid., 305.
16. *Niles Weekly Register*, September 20, 1828.
17. *Connecticut Courant*, April 27, 1830.
18. Ibid.
19. Letter, John C. Calhoun to S. D. Ingham, November 1832.
20. Bartlett, *John C. Calhoun*, 192–93.
21. "Speech on the Force Bill," in *Union and Liberty: The Political Philosophy of John C. Calhoun*, ed. Ross M. Lence (Indianapolis: Liberty Fund, 1992), 430–31.
22. Letter, John C. Calhoun to Edward North, November 33, 1833.
23. Coit, *John C. Calhoun*, 421.
24. Bartlett, *John C. Calhoun*, 377.
25. Ibid.
26. *Abridgment of the Debates of Congress, from 1789 to 1856* (New York: D. Appleton, 1861), 16:471–72.
27. Ibid., 472.
28. "Statue of John C. Calhoun Erected in Statuary Hall," The Capitol, Washington (1910), 15.

29 Coit, *John C. Calhoun*, 531.
30 Kirk, *The Conservative Mind*, 184.

Chapter 4: Grover Cleveland

1 Walters, *The Last Jeffersonian*, 20.
2 James McPherson, *Abraham Lincoln and the Second American Revolution* (New York: Oxford University Press, 1990), 128.
3 Allan Nevins, *Grover Cleveland: A Study in Courage* (New York: Dodd Mead, 1932), 157.
4 John M. Pafford, *The Forgotten Conservative* (Washington, DC: Regnery Publishing, 2013), 27.
5 *New York Tribune*, January 9, 1885.
6 Nevins, *Grover Cleveland*, 210.
7 Grover Cleveland, "Inaugural Address," March 4, 1885, *Messages and Papers of the Presidents* (New York: Bureau of National Literature, 1897), 10:4883–84.
8 Ibid., 4886.
9 Ibid., 4887.
10 Ibid., 4888.
11 Nevins, *Grover Cleveland*, 5.
12 Grover Cleveland, "Veto Message," February 16, 1887, *Messages and Papers of the Presidents*, 11:6142.
13 Ibid.
14 Grover Cleveland, "Third Annual Message," December 6, 1887, *Messages and Papers of the Presidents*, 11:5166.
15 Robert McElroy, *Grover Cleveland: The Man and the Statesman* (New York: Harper and Brothers, 1923), 271.
16 *New York Herald*, November 15, 1888.
17 Grover Cleveland, "The Principles of True Democracy," January 8, 1891, Philadelphia. See Nevins, *Grover Cleveland*, 464.
18 Grover Cleveland, "Letter to the Reform Club," February 1891. See Nevins, *Grover Cleveland*, 467.
19 Letter, Grover Cleveland to J. M. Russell, February 19, 1891.
20 Robert L. O'Brien, *Boston Evening Transcript*, June 27, 1908.
21 Nevins, *Grover Cleveland*, 510.
22 Grover Cleveland, "Inaugural Address," March 4, 1893, *Messages and Papers of the Presidents*, 12:5821.
23 Ibid., 5822.
24 Ibid., 5825.

CHAPTER 5: CALVIN COOLIDGE AND ANDREW MELLON

25 Henry F. Graff, *Grover Cleveland* (New York: Henry Holt, 2002), 138.
26 Nevins, *Grover Cleveland*, 764.

1 This quote was reported by several sources, including Senator George Pepper of Pennsylvania and presidential portrait artist Charles Hopkinson.
2 Paul Johnson, *A History of the American People* (New York: HarperCollins, 1997), 655.
3 Frederick Lewis Allen, *Only Yesterday* (New York: Harper & Row, 1931), 108.
4 *New Republic*, March 1921.
5 David Greenberg, *Calvin Coolidge* (New York: Henry Holt, 2006), 31.
6 Ibid., 32–33.
7 Calvin Coolidge, *The Autobiography of Calvin Coolidge* (New York: Cosmopolitan, 1929), 158.
8 Johnson, *A History of the American People*, 709.
9 Ibid., 712.
10 Amity Shlaes, *Coolidge* (New York: Harper, 2013), 9.
11 Calvin Coolidge, "Acceptance Speech," August 14, 1924, in *Foundations of the Republic: Speeches and Addresses* (New York: Scribner, 1926), 223.
12 Walter Lippmann, *Men of Destiny* (New York: Macmillan, 1927), 13.
13 Greenberg, *Calvin Coolidge*, 60.
14 David Cannadine, *Mellon: An American Life* (New York: Knopf, 2006), 310.
15 Ibid., 293.
16 Representative Simon D. Fess, Speech in the U.S. House of Representatives, December 7, 1922.
17 Shlaes, *The Forgotten Man*, 38.
18 Andrew Mellon, *Taxation: The People's Business* (New York: Macmillan, 1924), 126.
19 Cannadine, *Mellon*, 316.
20 Calvin Coolidge, "Inaugural Address," March 4, 1925, in *Messages and Papers of the Presidents*, 18:9481.
21 Cannadine, *Mellon*, 314.

22 Calvin Coolidge, Speech on the White House Grounds, August 11, 1924. According to the Internet Archive, this speech marked the first time a president was filmed with sound recording. See archive.org/details/coolidge_1924.
23 Cannadine, *Mellon*, 314.
24 See Garland S. Tucker III, *The High Tide of American Conservatism: Davis, Coolidge, and the 1924 Election* (Austin, TX: Emerald, 2010), 9.
25 Calvin Coolidge, Annual State of the Union Address, December 8, 1925, in *Messages and Papers of the Presidents*, 18:9514.
26 *Washington Post*, December 4, 1924.
27 Calvin Coolidge, "Speech to American Society of Newspaper Editors," January 17, 1925, in *Messages and Papers of the Presidents*, 18:9476.
28 Calvin Coolidge, "Inaugural Address," March 4, 1925, in *Messages and Papers of the Presidents*, 18:9481.
29 *Washington Post*, March 5, 1925.
30 Silver, *Coolidge and the Historians*, 111.
31 Johnson, *A History of the American People*, 718.
32 Silver, *Coolidge and the Historians*, 130.
33 Veronique de Rugy, "1920s Income Tax Cuts Sparked Economic Growth and Raised Federal Revenues," Cato Institute, March 4, 2003.
34 Calvin Coolidge, "Veto Message," *Messages and Papers of the Presidents*, 28:9658.
35 Ibid.
36 Ibid., 9687.
37 Shlaes, *Coolidge*, 9.
38 Calvin Coolidge, Speech on September 17, 1928, *Messages and Papers of the Presidents*, 28:9689.
39 Calvin Coolidge, Speech before Amherst College Alumni Association, February 6, 1916, in *Foundations of the Republic*, 187.
40 Calvin Coolidge, Address at Community Chest Dinner, Springfield, Massachusetts, October 11, 1921.
41 Calvin Coolidge, "The Things That Are Unseen," speech delivered June 19, 1923.
42 Cannadine, *Mellon*, 456.
43 *Pittsburgh Post-Gazette*, August 28, 1937.
44 *New York Times*, January 6, 1933.
45 Henry L. Mencken, *A Carnival of Buncombe* (Baltimore: Johns Hopkins Press, 1956), 61.

Chapter 6: Josiah W. Bailey

1. Letter, Bailey to editor of the *Madison Herald*, March 25, 1914, in the Josiah William Bailey Papers, Duke University (hereafter Bailey Papers).
2. Letter, Bailey to O. Max Gardner, November 11, 1927, Bailey Papers.
3. Letter, Bailey to G. S. Johnson, June 23, 1930, Bailey Papers.
4. *Charlotte Observer*, July 2, 1923.
5. *The Nation*, January 7, 1931, 78.
6. Letter, Bailey to Thurman Kitchin, October 28, 1935, Bailey Papers.
7. Letter, Bailey to Angus McLean, February 6, 1931, Bailey Papers.
8. *News and Observer*, April 19, 1932.
9. *New York Times*, February 10, 1937.
10. Josiah W. Bailey, "The Supreme Court, the Constitution, and the People," *Vital Speeches of the Day* (New York: City News Publishing, 1937), 3:290–95. See John Robert Moore, *Senator Josiah William Bailey of North Carolina* (Durham, NC: Duke University Press, 1968), 131.
11. Moore, *Senator Josiah William Bailey*, 133.
12. *New York Times*, June 21, 1938.
13. James T. Patterson, *Congressional Conservatism and the New Deal* (Lexington: University of Kentucky Press, 1967), 19.
14. Ibid., 20.
15. Ibid., 95.
16. Moore, *Senator Josiah William Bailey*, 137.
17. *New York Times*, March 31, 1937.
18. *New York Times*, November 2, 1937.
19. Letter, Bailey to O. L. Moore, November 6, 1937, Bailey Papers.
20. Letter, Bailey to David Lawrence, December 20, 1937, Bailey Papers.
21. *New York Times*, December 16, 1937. See also John Robert Moore, "Josiah W. Bailey and the 'Conservative Manifesto' of 1937," *Journal of Southern History* 31, no. 1 (February 1965): 34.
22. *New York Times*, December 17, 1937.
23. *Washington Post*, December 17, 1937.
24. *Congressional Record*, 75th Congress, 2nd session, 1936.
25. Letter, Bailey to Merwin Hart, February 22, 1938, Bailey Papers.
26. Henry Morgenthau Jr., "Revenue Review Hearings," 1939, FDR Presidential Library Papers.
27. *News and Observer*, December 16, 1946.
28. Ibid.
29. *News and Observer*, February 17, 1937.

Chapter 7: John W. Davis

1. Tucker, *The High Tide of American Conservatism*, 276.
2. John W. Davis, speech to the American Bar Association, 1935.
3. Tucker, *The High Tide of American Conservatism*, 103–4.
4. William Harbaugh, *Lawyer's Lawyer* (New York: Oxford University Press, 1973), 20.
5. John W. Davis, "Reminiscences by John W. Davis," Columbia University Oral History Project (1954), 31.
6. Ibid., 34.
7. Ibid., 85–86.
8. Harbaugh, *Lawyer's Lawyer*, 101.
9. Ibid., 106.
10. Ibid., 101–2.
11. *The Ambassadorial Diary of John W. Davis*, ed. Julia Davis and Dolores Fleming (Morgantown: West Virginia University Press, 1993), 216.
12. Robert Szold, "Interview," John W. Davis Collection, Washington and Lee University. See also Harbaugh, *Lawyer's Lawyer*, 103.
13. Letter, John W. Davis to John J. Davis, January 14, 1915, quoted in Frederick A.O. Schwarz III, "The Political Career of John W. Davis" (Harvard University, unpublished dissertation, 1957), 76.
14. Lippmann, *Men of Destiny*, 25.
15. Tucker, *The High Tide of American Conservatism*, 271.
16. John W. Davis, *Party Government in the United States* (Princeton, NJ: Princeton University Press, 1929), 39.
17. Harbaugh, *Lawyer's Lawyer*, 339.
18. Letter, John W. Davis to Walter Lippmann, June 24, 1935. See Tucker, *The High Tide of American Conservatism*, 271–72.
19. *New York Times*, October 30, 1932.
20. *New York Times*, March 5, 1933.
21. Schwarz, "The Political Career of John W. Davis," 90.
22. Harbaugh, *Lawyer's Lawyer*, 346.
23. Schwarz, "The Political Career of John W. Davis," 90.
24. *New York Times*, July 11, 1934.
25. Harbaugh, *Lawyer's Lawyer*, 341.
26. *New York Post*, May 28, 1935.
27. Tucker, *The High Tide of American Conservatism*, 276.
28. Harbaugh, *Lawyer's Lawyer*, 349.
29. John W. Davis, "Address to New York State Bar Association," January 20, 1936.

30 *New York Herald Tribune*, May 13, 1952.
31 Harbaugh, *Lawyer's Lawyer*, 464.
32 *New York Herald Tribune*, May 13, 1952.
33 Harbaugh, *Lawyer's Lawyer*, 482.
34 John W. Davis, speech in Sea Girt, New Jersey, August 21, 1924. Text of speech in John W. Davis Papers, Sterling Library, Yale University.
35 Letter, John W. Davis to L. H. Wood, March, 1953.
36 *Time*, December 22, 1952.
37 Harbaugh, *Lawyer's Lawyer*, 495.
38 *Time*, December 22, 1952.
39 Alexander Bickel, *The Least Dangerous Branch* (Westport, CT: Praeger, 2002), 42.
40 Harbaugh, *Lawyer's Lawyer*, 518.
41 Lippmann, *Men of Destiny*, 25.

Chapter 8: Robert A. Taft

1 *Time*, January 29, 1940.
2 *New Haven Register*, February 10, 1910.
3 James T. Patterson, *Mr. Republican* (Boston: Houghton Mifflin, 1972), 54.
4 Russell Kirk and James McClellan, *The Political Principles of Robert A. Taft* (New Brunswick, NJ: Transaction Publishing, 2010), xiii.
5 Patterson, *Mr. Republican*, 176.
6 *Proceedings of Republican National Convention*, 1936.
7 Robert Taft, speech quoted in the *Cincinnati Enquirer*, April 2, 1936.
8 Robert Taft, speech quoted in the *Akron Beacon Journal*, November 2, 1938.
9 *Time*, January 29, 1940.
10 Robert Taft and T. V. Smith, *Foundations of Democracy: A Series of Debates* (New York: Knopf, 1939).
11 Kirk and McClellan, *The Political Principles of Robert A. Taft*, 30.
12 Tocqueville, *Democracy in America*, 175.
13 *Christian Science Monitor*, January 14, 1940.
14 Patterson, *Mr. Republican*, 213.
15 Turner Catledge, *My Life and "The Times"* (New York: Harper & Row, 1971), 118–19.
16 Ibid.

17 Allen Drury, *A Senate Journal* (New York: McGraw-Hill, 1963), 30.
18 Robert Taft, speech before the American Irish Historical Society of New York, May 2, 1942, printed in the *Congressional Record*, 77th Congress, 2nd session, vol. 88, 1622.
19 *Saturday Evening Post*, December 11, 1943.
20 Robert Taft, speech at Kenyon College, October 6, 1946, quoted in Patterson, *Mr. Republican*, 326.
21 John F. Kennedy, *Profiles in Courage* (New York: Harper & Row, 1961), 193, 203–4.
22 Robert Taft, speech to Yale Alumni, February 22, 1947.
23 Peter Hannaford, ed., *The Quotable Calvin Coolidge* (Bennington, VT: Images from the Past, 2001), 24.
24 *New York Times*, July 11, 1934.
25 Malcolm Moos, *The Republicans: A History of Their Party* (New York: Harper, 1956), 482.
26 Kennedy, *Profiles in Courage*, 193.
27 *Washington Post*, August 4, 1953.
28 Kennedy, *Profiles in Courage*, 195.
29 Kirk and McClellan, *The Political Principles of Robert A. Taft*, 4.

Chapter 9: William F. Buckley Jr., Barry Goldwater, and Ronald Reagan

1 Lionel Trilling, *The Liberal Imagination* (New York: Harper, 1950), ix.
2 *American Political Science Review* (1952): 48.
3 Carl T. Bogus, *Buckley: William F. Buckley Jr. and the Rise of American Conservatism* (New York: Bloomsbury Press, 2011), 59.
4 William F. Buckley Jr., *God and Man at Yale* (Washington, DC: Regnery, 2002), xi.
5 Ibid., xxxii.
6 Ibid., 86.
7 Bogus, *Buckley*, 83.
8 Lee Edwards, *William F. Buckley Jr.: The Maker of a Movement* (Wilmington, DE: ISI Books, 2010), 44.
9 Ibid., 47.
10 By 1955 Buckley was using the term *conservatism* rather than the *individualism* that he had used in *God and Man at Yale*. The publication of Russell Kirk's *The Conservative Mind* in 1953 had had a substantial impact on Buckley and many others.

11 Edwards, *William F. Buckley Jr.*, 61.
12 Ibid., 76.
13 Barry Goldwater, *With No Apologies* (New York: Penguin, 1979), 44.
14 Robert A. Goldberg, *Barry Goldwater* (New Haven, CT: Yale University Press, 1995), 95.
15 Ibid., 98.
16 Barry Goldwater, *The Conscience of a Conservative* (Washington, DC: Regnery, 1990), 17.
17 *New York Times*, April 28, 1957.
18 Goldberg, *Barry Goldwater*, 116.
19 Bogus, *Buckley*, 191.
20 Patrick J. Buchanan, introduction to Goldwater, *The Conscience of a Conservative*, ix.
21 Goldwater, *The Conscience of a Conservative*, 61.
22 Goldberg, *Barry Goldwater*, 178.
23 Ibid.
24 *New York Times*, November 23, 1963.
25 Rick Perlstein, *Before the Storm* (New York: Hill and Wang, 2001), 204.
26 J. William Middendorf II, *A Glorious Disaster* (New York: Basic Books, 2006), 120–21.
27 Perlstein, *Before the Storm*, 381.
28 Ibid., 374.
29 William F. Buckley Jr., *Flying High* (New York: Basic Books, 2008), 151.
30 Middendorf, *A Glorious Disaster*, 133.
31 Lee Edwards, *Goldwater: The Man Who Made a Revolution* (Washington, DC: Regnery 1995), 114.
32 Middendorf, *A Glorious Disaster*, 208.
33 Buckley, *Flying High*, 180.
34 *New York Times*, November 5, 1964.
35 Buckley, *Flying High*, 180.
36 Middendorf, *A Glorious Disaster*, 221.
37 Arthur M. Schlesinger Jr., *History of American Presidential Elections, 1789–1968* (Boston: Houghton-Mifflin, 1969), 772.
38 William F. Buckley Jr., *Let Us Talk of Many Things* (Roseville, CA: Prima Forum, 2000), 76–78.
39 Buckley, *Flying High*, 191.
40 Goldberg, *Barry Goldwater*, 237.
41 *National Review*, March 24, 2008.

42 Edwards, *William F. Buckley Jr.*, 105.
43 William F. Buckley Jr., *The Reagan I Knew* (New York: Basic Books, 2008), 70.
44 *Ronald Reagan: A Life in Words and Pictures* (New York: Time-Life, 2005), 44.
45 Ibid., 56.
46 Steven F. Hayward, *The Age of Reagan: The Conservative Counterrevolution: 1980–1989* (New York: Crown Forum, 2009), 72.
47 *New York Times*, August 30, 1981.
48 Peggy Noonan, *When Character Was King* (New York: Viking, 2001), 222.
49 Ibid., 226.
50 Ibid., 42.
51 Ronald Reagan, speech at the Brandenburg Gate, Berlin, June 12, 1987.
52 Buckley, *The Reagan I Knew*, xx.
53 Noonan, *When Character Was King*, 94.
54 Buckley, *The Reagan I Knew*, 241.
55 Bogus, *Buckley*, 339.
56 *The Economist*, June 14, 2014, 24.
57 *National Review*, June 28, 2004, 16.
58 Noonan, *When Character Was King*, 317.

Acknowledgments

Editor Jed Donahue at ISI Books has been a pleasure to work with. He was consistently diligent, constructive, and patient in preparing this manuscript for publication. His counsel was invariably appropriate and wise. Elizabeth Brake, Duke University PhD and independent researcher, provided very able research assistance throughout the writing process and offered keen, constructive insights on many aspects of this book. As in everything over our forty-three years of married life, my wife, Greyson, was a source of invaluable encouragement, constructive oversight, and convivial companionship—for all of which I am very, very grateful.

Grateful acknowledgment is made for the following images used in this book:

- p. 27: (left) *Thomas Jefferson* by Mather Brown (1786), courtesy of the National Portrait Gallery, Smithsonian Institution, available from the Library of Congress; (right) *James Madison* by John Vanderlyn (1816), available from Wikimedia Commons
- p. 45: (left) *Nathaniel Macon* (c.1820), collection of the U.S. House of Representatives; (right) *John Randolph* by John Wesley Jarvis (1811), available from Wikimedia Commons
- p. 61: *John C. Calhoun* by George Peter Alexander Healy (c.1845), available from Wikimedia Commons
- p. 77: Grover Cleveland, photo by Napoleon Sarony (1892), available from the Library of Congress
- p. 97: Calvin Coolidge and Andrew Mellon (detail), photo by Harris & Ewing (1928), available from the Library of Congress
- p. 119: Senator Josiah W. Bailey, photo by Harris & Ewing (1940), available from the Library of Congress
- p. 137: John W. Davis, photo by Harris & Ewing (date unknown), available from the Library of Congress
- p. 157: Senator Robert Taft, photo by Harris & Ewing (1938 or 1939), available from the Library of Congress
- p. 173: (left) William F. Buckley Jr. (early 1950s), from the ISI archives; (center) Barry Goldwater, © 1964 by Vander White/Corbis; (right) Ronald Reagan (1981), available from the Library of Congress
- p. 198: Reagan, Goldwater, and Buckley (detail), © 1975 by Bettmann/Corbis

Index

Adams, Henry, 53, 58
Adams, John, 22, 37, 40, 50
Adams, John Quincy, 64
Agricultural Adjustment Act, 149
Alien and Sedition Acts, 40–43, 46–47
Allen, Frederick Lewis, 99
American Bar Association, 142, 150
American Liberty League, 147, 148
American Mercury, 177
American Revolution: Founders' view of human nature and, 20
"American System," 62
Annapolis Convention, 30–31

Articles of Confederation, 29, 30
Ashburn, Frank, 177

Bailey, Josiah W.: biographical overview and early political career, 120–21; Conservative Manifesto and the bipartisan coalition, 120, 128–35; death, legacy, and final words of, 135–36; in the history of conservatism, 25; "Holy Joe" sobriquet, 121; opposition to FDR's court-packing scheme, 124–25, 127, 151; personal characteristics and principles of, 121–22; on the "Roosevelt Recession," 128;

Bailey, Josiah W. (*cont'd*): support for FDR in 1932, 122–23
Baker, Newton D., 17, 144
Bank of the United States, 37–39, 55, 56
Barkley, Alben, 132, 168
Beame, Abe, 192
Biblical Recorder, 120
bill of rights: Jefferson and, 33
Blaine, James G., 80, 81, 91
Bogus, Carl, 182
Boston police strike (1919), 99–100, 116
Bozell, L. Brent, Jr., 182
Bramwell, Austin, 176
Brandeis, Louis, 149
Briggs v. Elliott, 153–56
Broder, David, 189
Brown, Edmund "Pat," 192
Bryan, William Jennings, 24, 94, 95
Buchan, John (Lord Tweedsmuir), 202
Buchanan, Pat, 182
Buckley, William F., Jr.: assessment of Reagan's impact, 199; combined conservative influence of Buckley, Goldwater, and Reagan, 199–200; emergence of the conservative movement and, 181; founding of Young Americans for Freedom, 179; goals for the *National Review*, 177–78; *God and Man at Yale*, writing of and reaction to, 174–77; on Goldwater's 1964 Republican nomination acceptance speech, 187; Goldwater's *The Conscience of a Conservative* and, 182; in the history of conservatism, 25; leadership at the *National Review*, 178; New York mayoral election of 1966, 191–92; on Reagan versus Ford in 1976, 193; response to Goldwater's defeat in 1964, 190–91; as a spokesman for conservatism, 178–79
Buckley, William F., Sr., 174
Bulkley, Robert J., 161–62
Bundy, McGeorge, 176–77
Burke, Edmund, 23
Burke, Edward R., 132
Burr, Aaron, 53
Bush, George H. W., 196
Byrd, Harry F.: 1930s bipartisan coalition and the Conservative Manifesto, 125, 126, 128, 129, 135; on Josiah Bailey, 124, 135; presidential election of 1932 and, 144
Byrnes, James, 153, 154

Calhoun, John C.: "Cast-Iron Man" sobriquet, 73; defense of limited government, 65–68; "dueling toasts" at the Jefferson Day dinner of 1830, 70–71; evaluations and legacy of, 74–76, 171; in the history of conservatism, 24; nullification and, 68–69, 72–73; John Randolph's influence on, 63; slavery and, 73–74; "South Carolina Exposition and Protest," 65–69; tariff battles, 61–73
Carter, Jimmy, 193–94
Catledge, Turner, 164–65
Chamberlain, John, 178

Chambers, Whittaker, 178
Chase, Samuel, 53
Churchill, Winston, 25, 202
civility: in politics, 202
civil service reform, 82, 85
Civil War: expansion of government during, 77–78; veterans' pensions, 85–86
"classical liberalism," 17
Clay, Henry, 62, 72, 74–75, 171
Cleveland, Grover: economy in government and, 83–84, 93; the "government should not support the people" principle and policies, 85–87; in the history of conservatism, 24; inaugural address of 1885, 83–85; inaugural address of 1893, 92–93; initial key policies as president, 81–83; interregnum between presidencies, 89; later career and legacy of, 95–96; Panic of 1893 and, 93–94; presidential election of 1884, 79–81; presidential election of 1888, 88–89; presidential election of 1892, 89–92; pursuit of governmental and civil service reform, 80, 82, 84, 85; schism in the Democratic Party in the 1890s and, 94–95; silver coinage and currency issues, 82, 89, 90–91, 92, 94; strict constructionism and, 80, 93; tariff reduction and, 82–83, 84, 87–89, 94; "The Principles of True Democracy" speech, 89–90
Coit, Margaret, 64
Cold War: Reagan and, 197, 198
Commager, Henry Steele, 19

Confederation Congress, 29
Conscience of a Conservative, The (Goldwater), 18, 182–83, 200
conservatism: Buckley and, 174–79; evolution of term, 17–18; foundational principles, 18–23; historical overview, 23–25; importance of ideas, 201–2; state of in the early 1950s, 173–74. *See also* conservative movement
conservative Democrats: Josiah Bailey's bipartisan coalition and the Conservative Manifesto, 120, 127–35; John Davis's opposition to the New Deal, 137–38, 146–51 (*see also* Davis, John W.); opposition to FDR's court-packing scheme, 123–27, 151; Robert Taft's bipartisan conservative coalition and, 163, 166. *See also* Cleveland, Grover
Conservative Manifesto, 120; Josiah Bailey's defense of in the Senate, 132–33; failure of the Senate to endorse, 133–34; influence of, 134–35; origins of, 127–30; press coverage following the leak of, 132; principles presented in, 130–32
Conservative Mind, The (Kirk), 18
conservative movement: Buckley and, 174–79, 181; combined influence of Buckley, Goldwater, and Reagan, 199–200; elections of 1966, 191–92; emergence of, 181; Goldwater's *The Conscience of a Conservative* and, 182–83;

conservative movement (*cont'd*): presidential campaign and election of 1964, 183–88; Reagan as a conservative spokesman while governor of California, 192–93; Reagan's political debut during the Goldwater campaign, 188–89; Reagan's presidency, 194–99; response to Goldwater's defeat in 1964, 190–91

Constitutional Convention, 30–33

Coolidge, Calvin: belief in and implementation of conservative principles as president, 112–15; Boston police strike as governor of Massachusetts, 99–100, 116; death, funeral, and praise of, 116–17; economic policy and tax reform, 103, 104, 105–10; economic prosperity in the 1920s and, 110; in the history of conservatism, 24; influence on Reagan, 195, 196; Ku Klux Klan issue of 1924 and, 154; liberal and conservative historians on, 19; major addresses on economy and taxation as moral issues, 106–10; opposition to the McNary-Haugen Farm Relief Bill and the idea of equalization, 111–12; partnership with Mellon, 103, 104, 105–6, 109, 110; philosophy of intentional inaction, 100, 101–2; presidential election of 1924 and, 106; rise to the presidency, 97–98; Robert Taft's conservatism and, 170;

"The chief business of the American people is business" misquote, 107; as vice president, 97, 99, 100–101

Coolidge and the Historians (Silver), 18–19

corruption: the postbellum Republican Party and, 79

currency issues: Cleveland and, 82, 89, 90–91, 92, 94

Davis, Anna, 138

Davis, John J., 138

Davis, John W.: ambassador to the Court of St. James's, 142; assessment of Hoover's presidency, 144–45; attack on the Ku Klux Klan, 153–54; belief in Jeffersonian principles, 141, 143–44, 145, 146; death of and praise for, 156; early political career, 139–40; education in law and early conservative influences on, 138–39; FDR labels "Public Enemy Number One," 137, 150; in the history of conservatism, 25; last cases argued before the Supreme Court, 151–56; on liberty, 22; offered a Supreme Court position in 1922, 142; opposition to FDR's court-packing scheme, 151; opposition to the New Deal, 137–38, 146–51; parents of, 138; personal philosophy of, 147; presidential election of 1924 and, 106, 142–43; private law career, 139, 142, 143; sobriquets, 137; as solicitor general under Wilson,

140–42; Stafford Little Lectures on political philosophy, 143–44; support for Al Smith in 1928, 144; support for FDR in 1932, 144, 145–46; Robert Taft's conservatism and, 170; testifying before congressional committees, 143
Democratic Party: Cleveland's rise to the presidency in 1884, 79–81 (*see also* Cleveland, Grover); free silver and, 90–91; heir to the Jeffersonian Republicans, 77; liberal dominance of in the early 1950s, 173–74; Mugwumps, 79, 80; opposition to tariff reform, 88; presidential election of 1924, 142–43; presidential election of 1932, 119; reemergence in the late 1800s, 79; schism in the 1890s, 94–95; state of prior to and following the Civil War, 77, 78–79. *See also* conservative Democrats
Democratic-Republicans, 64
Dewey, Thomas, 165
Dissertation on Slavery, A (Tucker), 51
Dodd, William E., 47
Douglas, Lewis W., 128
Draft Goldwater for President Committee, 184, 191
Drury, Allen, 166

economic equality, 22
economy in government: Cleveland and, 83–84, 93; Coolidge on, 107–8
Edison Electric Institute, 149

Edwards, Lee, 177, 188
Eisenhower, Dwight D., 181, 186
equalization, 111–12

Fair Deal, 174
Federalist Papers, The, 20, 35–37
Federalists: John Adams's administration and the Alien and Sedition Acts controversy, 40–43; John Adams's "midnight appointments," 50; Constitutional Convention and, 30–31; demise of, 77; emergence of, 30; impeachment of Samuel Chase and, 53; Jefferson's attempt to separate Madison from, 34; national bank issue, 37–39; "Revolution of 1800," 43, 45; views of Congressional representation, 50
federal judiciary, 50
"Five Greatest Senators in U.S. History," 171–72
Force Bill, 71, 72
Ford, Gerald, 193
Foundations of Democracy (Taft), 162–63
Founders: on human nature, 20; on the limits of government, 21; on property rights and human rights, 21–22
France, 20, 40
Frazier-Lemke Act, 149
free trade, 56
French Revolution, 20

Garner, John Nance, 127, 132
Garrison, William Lloyd, 74
Gascoyn-Cecil, Robert (Lord Salisbury), 101

Glass, Carter, 125–26, 128
God and Man at Yale (Buckley), 174–77
Goldberg, Robert, 181–82
gold standard, 82, 90, 94
Goldwater, Barry: combined conservative influence of Buckley, Goldwater, and Reagan, 199–200; *The Conscience of a Conservative*, 18, 182–83; as a conservative leader and spokesman, 181–83; early political career, 180–81; in the history of conservatism, 25, 179; JFK's assassination and, 184; presidential campaign and election of 1964, 183–88; response of conservatives to the 1964 defeat, 190–91
government: expansion and interventionism under the New Deal, 24–25, 119–20, 123; expansion during the Civil War, 77–78; primary roles of, 20–21. *See also* economy in government; limited government
graciousness: in politics, 202
Grand Old Party (GOP), 78. *See also* Republican Party
Graves, Charles A., 139
Green, Duff, 69
Greenberg, David, 100
Griswold, Whitney, 176

Hamilton, Alexander: Constitutional Convention and, 30–31; *The Federalist Papers* and, 35; Federalists and, 30; national bank issue and the concept of "implied powers," 37, 38, 39; on property rights and liberty, 22; tariff issues and, 55; view of human nature, 20
Hand, Learned, 153
Harding, Warren: conservative policies as president, 101; John Davis and, 142; death of and Coolidge's rise to the presidency, 97–98, 102; in the history of conservatism, 24; presidential election of 1920, 98–99, 100–101
"Hard Way, The" (Bailey), 124
Harrison, Benjamin, 88, 91, 92
Hayne, Robert Y., 64, 69–70
Henry, Patrick, 20
Hewitt, Abraham, 82
Hicks, Granville, 23
historians: liberal, 18–19
history: importance of studying, 202
Hoover, Herbert, 24, 115, 119, 122, 144–45
Hughes, Charles Evans, 140
human nature: conservatism and, 20; John Randolph's view of, 58
human rights: conservatism and, 21–22
"Hundred Days," 123

Ickes, Harold, 150
ideas: importance of, 201–2
impeachment: of Samuel Chase, 53
"implied powers" concept, 37
income tax reform. *See* tax reform
Intercollegiate Society of Individualists, 177

Intercollegiate Studies Institute, 177
interposition, 42, 68, 69

Jackson, Andrew, 64, 65, 70–72
Jay, John, 35
Jay Treaty, 46
Jefferson, Thomas: analysis of the Constitution in 1787, 33–34; appointed first secretary of state, 37; attempts to separate Madison from the Federalists, 34; bill of rights and, 33; on the code of silence at the Philadelphia convention, 32; differences with Madison over the Constitution, 34; elected vice president, 40; first term as president, 49–50; friendship and political collaboration with Madison, 27–29; in the history of conservatism, 23; Kentucky Resolution and the Alien and Sedition Acts controversy, 41–43; on the limits of government, 21; Nathaniel Macon and, 47, 52–53; national bank issue and the birth of strict constructionism, 37, 38; nullification concept and, 42; John Randolph's split with, 52–53; response to the Shays's Rebellion, 29
Jefferson Day dinner (of 1830), 70–71
Jeffersonian Republicans: abandonment of true Republican principles, 56–57; Alien and Sedition Acts controversy, 40–43; anti-Federalist positions of Nathaniel Macon, 46–47; Congressional actions during Jefferson's first term as president, 49–50; friendship and political collaboration of Nathaniel Macon and John Randolph, 45–46, 47, 48–49; "Old Republicans," 54–57; John Randolph as House floor leader, 45, 49, 52; John Randolph's and Nathaniel Macon's split with, 52–55; "Revolution of 1800," 43, 45; states' rights and noninterference in slavery, 50–52
John Paul II, Pope, 198
Johnson, Hiram, 98
Johnson, Lyndon, 25, 184, 187, 188, 189
Johnson, Paul, 19, 99, 101, 110
judicial activism, 156
judicial review, 47

Kennedy, John F., 169, 171, 184, 185
Kentucky Resolution, 41–43, 46–47, 68
Kirk, Russell: *The Conservative Mind*, 18; on the importance of religion, 23; at the *National Review*, 178; on John Randolph, 51, 52, 54–55, 58; on the "Republican principles of 1800," 57; on the significance of Randolph and Calhoun, 76; on Robert Taft, 158, 163, 172; on the *Tertium Quids*, 54
Ku Klux Klan, 153–54

Laffer Curve, 104
La Follette, Robert M., 104, 171
Lamar, Joseph, 140
Landon, Alf, 160, 161
legislating: John Randolph's views of, 54–55
liberal historians, 18–19
liberalism: meanings of, 17
liberty: John Davis on, 22; government and, 20–21; Hamilton on property rights and liberty, 22; Robert Taft and, 163, 166–67, 172
Liberty League. *See* American Liberty League
limited government: Calhoun's defense of, 65–68; conservatism's views on, 21; Nathaniel Macon on, 47; Madison on, 35–36; John Randolph and Nathaniel Macon's defense of, 55–57; Reagan on, 195
Lindsay, John, 192
Lippmann, Walter, 102, 142–43, 144–45, 151, 156, 190
Locke, John, 21–22
Lodge, Henry Cabot, 75–76, 186
Longworth, Alice Roosevelt, 164
Lord, Herbert Mayhew, 113
Louisiana Purchase, 53
Louisville v. Radford, 149
Lowden, Frank, 98–99
Lubell, Samuel, 170–71

Macdonald, Dwight, 177
Macon, Nathaniel: anti-Federalist positions, 46–47; biographical overview, 46; character and legacy of, 58–59; friendship and political collaboration with John Randolph, 45–46, 47, 48–49, 57, 59; in the history of conservatism, 23; as a member of the *Tertium Quids*, 54; opposition to the extension of federal power, 55–57; split with the Jeffersonian Republicans, 52–53, 54; views of slavery, 50–52; views of the meaning of representation, 50
Madison, James: Annapolis Convention and, 30–31; Confederation Congress and, 29; differences with Jefferson over the Constitution, 34; as "Father of the Constitution," 32; *The Federalist Papers* and, 35–37; in the First Congress, 37; friendship and political collaboration with Jefferson, 27–29; in the history of conservatism, 23; interposition concept and, 42; Jefferson's attempt to separate from the Federalists, 34; on limited national government, 35–36; Nathaniel Macon and, 46, 47, 53; national bank issue and the birth of strict constructionism, 37–39; opposition to the Jay Treaty, 46; John Randolph's split with, 53; response to the Shays's Rebellion, 29–30; summary of the goals of the Constitutional Convention, 32–33; views on economic equality, 22; Virginia Plan and, 31–32; Virginia Resolution and the Alien and Sedition Acts controversy, 41, 42–43

Manion, Clarence, 181, 182
Marshall, Thurgood, 154, 155
McAdoo, William G., 142
McClellan, James, 158, 163
McClosky, Herbert, 173
McFarland, Ernest, 180
McKinley, William, 95
McKinley Tariff, 89, 90, 94
McNary, Charles, 129–30, 157
McNary-Haugen Farm Relief Bill, 111–12
McPherson, James, 78
McReynolds, James Clark, 140
Mellon, Andrew W.: belief in "commonsense government," 113; business career and wealth of, 102; FDR's tax investigation of, 116; fiscal policy and tax reform, 103–6; government service under Hoover, 115; in the history of conservatism, 24; opposition to the McNary-Haugen Farm Relief Bill, 111; partnership with Coolidge, 103, 104, 105–6, 109, 110; philanthropy of, 115–16; as Secretary of the Treasury, 102, 103
Mellon Plan, 103–4
Mencken, H. L., 117, 161, 177
"midnight appointments": of John Adams, 50
Monroe, James, 37
Morgenthau, Henry, Jr., 127–28, 134
"Mr. Jefferson's University" (Davis), 147–48
Mugwumps, 79, 80

national bank issue, 37–39, 55, 56
National Democratic Party, 95

National Review: Buckley's goals for, 177–78; Buckley's leadership at, 178; emergence of the conservative movement and, 181; Goldwater's 1964 Republican nomination acceptance speech and, 187; in the history of conservatism, 25
Nevins, Allan, 19, 79, 82, 84–85, 96
New Deal: Josiah Bailey's bipartisan coalition opposed to, 128–35; Josiah Bailey's support for in 1932, 122–23; John Davis's opposition to, 137–38, 146–51; governmental expansion and interventionism during, 24–25, 119–20, 123; liberalism and, 17; Robert Taft's bipartisan coalition opposed to, 166; Robert Taft's conservative philosophy and criticism of, 158–61
New Frontier, 184
Nixon, Richard, 193
Noonan, Peggy, 197
Norris, George, 109
nullification, 42; Calhoun, Jackson, and tariff controversies, 68–69, 71–73
Nuremberg Trials, 168–69

Obama, Barack, 25
O'Brian, John Lord, 141
Ohio, 51
Old Republicans, 54–57. *See also* Calhoun, John C.; Macon, Nathaniel; Randolph, John

order: government and, 20–21; Madison on, 35
O'Sullivan, John, 191, 199–200

Panic of 1893, 93–94
Parker, Alton, 95
Parker, John, 154
Party Government in the United States (Davis), 143–44
pensions. *See* veterans' pensions
personal liberty. *See* liberty
Philadelphia convention, 30–33
Phillips, Wendell, 74
Pierce, William, 32
politics: importance of graciousness and civility in, 202
"Principles of True Democracy, The" (Cleveland), 89–90
Professional Air Traffic Controllers Organization (PATCO) strike, 195–96
Profiles in Courage (Kennedy), 169, 171
property rights, 21–22
Public Utility Holding Company Act of 1935, 149–50
Publius essays, 35. *See also* Federalist Papers, The

Quasi-War, 40
Quids. *See* Tertium Quids

Randolph, Edmund, 31
Randolph, John: federal judiciary and, 50; friendship and political collaboration with Nathaniel Macon, 45–46, 47, 48–49, 57, 59; in the history of conservatism, 23; influence on Calhoun, 63; Russell Kirk on, 51, 52, 54–55, 58, 76; later career and legacy of, 57–58; as a member of the *Tertium Quids*, 54–55; opposition to tariffs, 62–63; opposition to the extension of federal power, 55–57; physical appearance, 47–48; as Republican floor leader, 45, 49, 52; split with the Jeffersonian Republicans, 52–54; views of human nature, 58; views of legislating, 54–55; views of slavery, 51, 52; views of the meaning of representation, 50
Reagan, Ronald: accomplishments as president, 195–99; combined conservative influence of Buckley, Goldwater, and Reagan, 199–200; as a conservative spokesman while governor of California, 192–93; elected governor of California, 191, 192; emergence of the conservative movement and, 181; first inaugural address, 194–95; in the history of conservatism, 25; the Laffer Curve and, 104; personal characteristics, 199; political debut during the Goldwater campaign, 188–89; presidential elections and, 193–94; response to Goldwater's defeat in 1964, 191
Reconstruction, 78
Reed, Thomas, 89, 90
reform: Cleveland and, 80, 84, 85; Mugwumps and, 79
representation: John Randolph's and Nathaniel Macon's views on, 50

Republican Party: 1930s bipartisan coalition and the Conservative Manifesto, 128–35; "billion-dollar Congress" of the late 1800s, 89; corruption and, 79; formation in 1860, 77; governmental expansion during and following the Civil War, 77–78; one-party rule following the Civil War, 78–79; presidential election of 1920, 98–101; presidential election of 1936, 157; presidential election of 1964, 183–88; pro-tariff platform and Harrison's election to the presidency, 88–89; state of conservatism in the early 1950s, 174; Robert Taft and the revival of conservatism in, 157, 163–64, 169–70; Robert Taft's bipartisan conservative coalition and, 163, 166; Robert Taft's campaigns for the presidency, 164–66, 170–71
"Republican principles of 1800," 57
Republic Steel company, 152
Reston, James, 189–90
Revenue Act of 1921, 105
Revenue Act of 1926, 109
"Revolution of 1800," 43, 45
Reynolds, Robert, 135
Robinson, Joseph, 127
Rockefeller, Nelson, 184, 185, 186
Roosevelt, Franklin Delano: Josiah Bailey's support for in 1932, 122–23; conservative opposition to the court-packing scheme of, 123–27, 151; John Davis and, 137, 144, 145–46, 150; governmental expansion and interventionism under the New Deal, 24–25, 119–20, 123 (*see also* New Deal); on the presidential election of 1924, 106; presidential election of 1932, 119; presidential election of 1936, 157; presidential election of 1940, 165; recession of 1937, 127–28; tax investigation of Mellon, 116
Roosevelt, Theodore, 98, 100
"Roosevelt Recession," 127–28

Salisbury, Lord (Robert Gascoyne-Cecil), 101
Saunders, W. O., 124
Schlesinger, Arthur, Jr., 18–19, 190
Scranton, William, 185–86
"Scranton letter," 185–86
segregation: *Briggs v. Elliott*, 153–56
Shays, Daniel, 29
Shays's Rebellion, 29–30
Sherman Silver Purchase Act, 89, 94
Shlaes, Amity, 17, 19, 101, 113
Shultz, George, 196
Silver, Thomas, 18–19, 109–10
silver coinage, 82, 89, 90–91, 94
Simmons, Furnifold M., 121
slavery: Calhoun and, 73–74; Jeffersonian Republican views of states' rights and noninterference, 50–52
Smith, Al, 121, 142, 144
Smith, T. V., 162
solicitor general, 140–42

South Carolina: segregation and the *Briggs v. Elliott* case, 153–56; tariff issues, 64, 68–69, 71, 72

"South Carolina Exposition and Protest" (Calhoun), 65–69

spiritual values: Coolidge and, 114

Stafford Little Lectures, 143–44

states and states' rights: Alien and Sedition Acts controversy, 41–43; Calhoun's defense of, 67–68; Jeffersonian Republicans and noninterference in slavery, 50–52; Nathaniel Macon on, 47; Madison on, 36; opposing views of Madison and Jefferson on, 34. *See also* interposition; nullification

Steel Seizure Case, 151–53

stock market crash (1929), 115, 119

strict constructionism: Calhoun and, 63; Cleveland and, 80, 93; national bank issue and the birth of, 37–39

supply-side income tax rate cuts, 110

Taft, Alphonso, 158

Taft, Robert A.: balance of order and freedom, 21; bipartisan conservative coalition formed by, 135, 163, 166; character sketch of, 164–65; conservative philosophy and criticism of the New Deal, 158–61; conservative predecessors, 170; conservative principles of, 162–63, 167–70; death and praise of, 171–72; education and private law career of, 158–59; elected senator from Ohio in 1938, 161–62; family history, 158; in the history of conservatism, 25; liberty and, 163, 166–67, 172; opposition to the Nuremberg Trials, 168–69; presidential campaigns of, 164–66, 170–71; presidential election of 1936 and, 160–61; revival of Republican conservatism and, 157, 163–64, 169–70

Taft, William Howard, 140, 142, 158

Taft-Hartley Act of 1947, 152, 195

Tammany Hall, 80, 91–92

tariffs: Calhoun and, 61–73; Cleveland and, 82–83, 84, 87–89, 94; McKinley Tariff, 89, 90, 94; nullification and, 68–69, 71–73; Old Republicans and, 55–56; postbellum Republicans and, 79; John Randolph and, 62–63; Tariff of 1816, 62; Tariff of 1828, the "Tariff of Abominations," 63–64; the Webster–Hayne debate of 1830, 69–70; Wilson-Gorman Tariff Act, 94

Taxation: The People's Business (Mellon), 103–4

tax reform: Coolidge-Mellon economic policy and, 105–10; economic prosperity in the 1920s and, 110; the Mellon

Plan, 103–4; Reagan and, 196–97
Tertium Quids, 54–57
Texas Seed Bill, 86–87
Thatcher, Margaret, 198
Thomas bill of 1943, 166
Thompson, Huston, 141
Tilden, Samuel J., 80, 82
Tocqueville, Alexis de, 22, 164
"Torch Democracy Keeps Alight, The" (Davis), 146
Trilling, Lionel, 173
Truman, Harry S., 152, 171, 174, 202
Tucker, John Randolph, 139
Tucker, St. George, 51
Tweedsmuir, Lord (John Buchan), 202

United States v. Butler, 148–49
United Steel Workers of America, 152
U.S. ambassador: John Davis as, 142
U.S. Constitution: *The Federalist Papers* and ratification of, 35–37; Jefferson's 1787 analysis of, 33–34; Madison's summary of the goals achieved by, 32–33; national bank issue and the birth of strict constructionism, 37–39; opposing views of Madison and Jefferson on, 34
U.S. Supreme Court: *Briggs v. Elliott*, 153–56; conservative opposition to FDR's court-packing scheme, 123–27, 151; John Davis as solicitor general under Wilson, 140–42;

John Davis's challenges to the New Deal, 138, 148–50; John Davis's last two cases before, 151–56; impeachment of Samuel Chase, 53; judicial activism and, 156; judicial review, 47; *Louisville v. Radford*, 149; states' rights and, Calhoun's analysis of, 67–68; *United States v. Butler*, 148–49; *Youngstown Sheet and Tube Co. v. Sawyer*, 151–53
U.S. Treasury, 82. *See also* Mellon, Andrew W.

Van Buren, Martin, 70
Vandenberg, Arthur, 129, 133
veterans' pensions, 85–86
Vinson, Fred, 155
Virginia Plan, 31–32
Virginia Resolution, 41, 42–43, 46–47, 68
virtues: importance of, 23

Warren, Earl, 155
Washington, George, 32, 37, 39
Webster, Daniel, 69–70, 74, 75, 151, 171
Wheeler, John, 47, 58, 59
Whigs, 77
White, Edward Douglass, 140–41
White, F. Clifton, 184, 191
White, Theodore, 187
"Why I Am a Democrat" (Davis), 145–46
Wicker, Tom, 190
Wilkie, Wendell, 165, 166
Wilson, John Q., 22
Wilson, Woodrow, 98, 121, 122, 140, 142

Wilson-Gorman Tariff Act, 94
Wood, Leonard, 98
World War II: Robert Taft's defense of personal liberty during, 166–67

Yale University, 174–77
Yates, Richard, 78
Young Americans for Freedom, 179, 190–91
Youngstown Sheet and Tube Co. v. Sawyer, 151–53

About the Author

Garland S. Tucker III is the author of *The High Tide of American Conservatism: Davis, Coolidge, and the 1924 Election*. He is retired chairman/CEO of Triangle Capital Corporation, a New York Stock Exchange–listed specialty finance company located in Raleigh, North Carolina. Tucker graduated magna cum laude and Phi Beta Kappa from Washington and Lee University and received his MBA from Harvard Business School.

INTERCOLLEGIATE STUDIES INSTITUTE

think. live free.™

ISI Books is the publishing imprint of the **Intercollegiate Studies Institute**.

Most thoughtful college students are sick of getting a shallow education in which too many viewpoints are shut out and rigorous discussion is shut down.

We teach them the principles of liberty and plug them into a vibrant intellectual community so that they get the collegiate experience they hunger for.

www.isi.org